How to Be Your Own Marriage Counselor

How to Be Your Own Marriage Counselor

Frieda Porat, Ph.D.
with
Henry Still

Rawson Associates Publishers, Inc.
New York

Library of Congress Cataloging in Publication Data

Porat, Frieda
How to be your own marriage counselor.

Bibliography: p. 261–263
Includes index.
1. Marriage. I. Still, Henry, joint author.
II. Title.
HQ734.P77   1977   301.42'7   77-88193
ISBN 0-89256-042-8

Copyright © 1978 by Frieda Porat, Ph.D.
All rights reserved
Published simultaneously in Canada by
McClelland and Stewart, Ltd.
Manufactured in the United States of America by
Fairfield Graphics, Fairfield, Pennsylvania
Designed by Gene Siegel
First Edition

To my husband,
Dan,
and to my children:
Marc Uri,
Ruth,
Naomi,

with all my love.

Acknowledgments

For assistance and encouragement in the writing of this book, I wish to acknowledge and thank all my students and the clients in my marriage counseling practice.

Especially, I wish to thank Betsy Taub for her fine assistance in editing; Sandi Gelles-Cole for editorial guidance; and my family for their support and patience.

Contents

*Introduction: You Don't Have to Lie on
Someone Else's Couch* — xi
1. The Myths about Marriage — 3
2. The Realities of Being Married — 15
3. Marriage Styles — 38
4. The Marital Check-Up — 54
5. Creative Communication and Conflict Resolution — 82
6. Sex: Myth and Reality — 110
7. Values and Meaning — 140
8. The Use of Time — 155
9. Managing Your Money — 174
10. Children — 191
11. Managing Friendships — 219
12. The Art of Negotiating Contracts — 235
13. What to Do When It Doesn't Work — 250

Bibliography — 261

Index — 264

Introduction
You Don't Have to Lie on Someone Else's Couch

My years of counseling many couples have made me keenly conscious of the high divorce rate in this country and the tremendous confusion during this state of flux regarding man/woman role definitions. I have also become aware of two other facts:

1. With all the marriage counselors available, we still can not possibly help all the couples needing our services. There just are not enough trained professionals to go around.
2. Not all couples can afford the rising rates of marriage counselors.

Because of these facts, and because it is possible for a couple to work on their relationship themselves, I want to make self-help available to couples who may need assistance.

In this book I have covered the major problem areas

that commonly complicate a couple relationship. By working through these areas methodically—separately and together—you can improve your relationship. This can apply to marriages that are already working well, as well as to those which appear to be headed for trouble.

What Is Marriage Counseling?

There is no specific magic attached to the profession of marriage counseling. A marriage counselor is a professional with a background in psychology. This person has earned an advanced degree and, in the process, has learned about family interaction and communication.

The marriage counselor sees the family as a system. He or she focuses on problem-solving with the couple and with the whole family. A marriage counselor is also trained in divorce counseling, premarital counseling, and sexual counseling. Basically the counselor works with healthy people who need help solving interpersonal problems.

Marriage counseling is designed to produce results in a relatively short period of time and therefore is less time-consuming and expensive than psychoanalytic involvement. On the average, a couple will see significant improvement after several months of marriage counseling.

The marriage counselor sees partners separately and together. The purpose is to help each person to see his own individual problems as well as the problems generated within the relationship. Counseling deals with problems *now;* it does not take you back to childhood problems. Psychoanalysis, on the other hand, does take you back to your early childhood and as in-depth therapy will take several years to complete.

The important point is that it is not necessary to lie on someone else's couch to solve some of your problems.

Introduction

We all need to have somebody listen to us in a nonjudgmental way. If you have a friend who is a good listener but not an advice giver, then you have a start. By hearing yourself express positive and negative feelings and thoughts, you learn about yourself and who you are.

If you don't have a willing listener available, then you have other options, such as: (1) talking into a tape recorder and replaying it to yourself, or (2) writing a journal and rereading it after a few days. If your partner is willing to be the listener, this is well and good. But it will be necessary for you both to develop the skills for expressing and receiving both positive and negative feelings about your relationship without damaging or destroying the good that you already have between you.

Finally, this book can be a "listener" and can teach you to be your own marriage counselor, because good counseling tells us how to change our old beliefs and attitudes—many of which by now may be outmoded fallacies. However, you must have a willing partner or you cannot have a healthy relationship. This book is for the *two* of you.

For Whom Is This Book Written?

I have written this for all couples involved in heterosexual relationships, for men and women. Although the title contains the word "marriage," a couple need not be formally married to benefit. The target groups for this information are:

1. Couples involved in a *living-together arrangement*. Because of the tenuousness of marriage these days, this arrangement has become both a popular alternative and a precursor to marriage.

2. Couples who are thinking of getting married and

want to start off right by learning some of the basics involved in a healthy marriage.

3. Married couples who, although not unhappy or disturbed in their relationship, wish to gain insight and achieve additional depth and excitement in their marriage.

4. Married couples who are experiencing problems in their relationship. Because they are uncomfortable, they feel a greater need to identify their problems and to find solutions.

What You Need to Benefit from This Book

A number of conditions are necessary for this book to work for you. Check yourself—and your partner—on the following five points:

1. *Am I willing to make a commitment to myself and to my partner to make changes?*

All too often I see people who say that they want to make changes, but when the going gets rough and there is work involved, they lose their enthusiasm. Let's not fool ourselves. *Change requires a lot of effort.*

2. *Do I admit to at least 50 percent of the responsibility for making our relationship work?*

If you are willing to read this book *only* to appease your partner, and believe it is really your partner who is causing most of the problems in your relationship, *save your energy!* This attitude does not contribute to a healthy partnership and the book probably will not help you.

3. *Am I willing to spend time alone and with my partner making discoveries and experimenting with changes?*

This is not a spicy novel to be flipped through in an evening or two. There's a lot of material here. If you take it too quickly, you may overload yourself and lose much

Introduction

of the benefit. By all means, use the book at your own speed, whether it be for two weeks or two months, but study and work with it thoroughly chapter by chapter. I suggest that you set aside a specific time in the day to read the book and perform the prescribed exercises, then *stick to those times.*

4. *Will I persevere in exploring areas which are uncomfortable and work out compromises with my partner?*

I have learned that it is precisely those areas which are the most difficult to explore that most need to be explored. You must not give up exploring at the first twinge of pain. Self-discovery, for you and your partner, can be a painful process, but also it can be most rewarding.

5. *Am I willing to expose my vulnerable areas and to agree with my partner that neither of us will take advantage of the other's vulnerabilities?*

This is an important point. You cannot have a close relationship without opening up and thus making yourself vulnerable to your partner. If you do so regularly, the fear of being hurt will diminish, but this will happen only if you trust each other not to take advantage of the "sore points," the areas of vulnerability. If your partner tries to use personal information against you, or to hurt you, he or she really cannot be considered a close friend. This breach in trust must be mended before any further progress can be made.

Will the Book Work for You?

It's really not the book that works; *you* make it work.

If you gave positive and sincere answers to the preceding five questions, then there are strong odds that working at the methods described in the following chapters will help you to improve your relationship.

INTRODUCTION

I share the same information with you here that you would receive if you were sitting in my office. Although we are not actually talking with each other, I hope this book will take the place of most of my side of the conversation. I ask many thought-provoking questions, and your response to those questions will encourage soul-searching, within yourself and with your partner.

Beyond soul-searching, this book will work best for you if you and your partner each keep a notebook. It is not sufficient merely to answer the questions to yourself as you are reading, but you need to write down a permanent record of your progress. This serves both to fix the exercises in your mind and to refresh your memory when you wish to "leaf back" and rediscover where you've been in your self-counseling.

I suggest a looseleaf binder so that extra pages may be inserted wherever you need them. Divide the binder into sections corresponding to chapters of this book. Then—at whatever speed is most comfortable for you and your partner—work through the book chapter by chapter. If you are not experiencing the problems discussed in one chapter, you may wish to move directly to the next.

Take as much time with each chapter as you feel you need to resolve those problems.

Do the exercises prescribed in each chapter.

As you do this, feel free to add any information, thoughts, or insights that come to you as you work.

By organizing your notebook chapter by chapter, you will be able to find the information readily when the time comes to go over it with your partner.

And remember—both of you—your workbook is like a diary or a journal. Make a contract at the beginning that neither of you will browse through your partner's notebook without permission. Trust is a must in any sharing or growth experience.

Introduction

How Do We Learn to Change?

Through previous questions, we have already tested your willingness to approach your own marriage counseling with an open mind. If you are willing to change your ways of thinking, then you are ready to change your actions and behaviors as well.

The hardest part is *practice*. Therefore, the workbook is your key to progress and change.

This book is totally oriented toward positive action. By encouraging direct assertiveness, you and your partner are guided to examine your relationship. You will ask each other direct, confronting questions, and practice new ways of relating to each other. Psychological change occurs when people are willing to solve their problems *now*—in the *present*—rather than dwelling on the past or trying to foresee the future.

How do we learn to change?
- By doing.
- By trying new ways.
- By observing.
- By sharing experiences.

This book can be a means of self-education and self-help. It can also be an effective and economical method for promoting growth and change in your relationship.

Some points to keep in mind as you begin:

Don't blame others for your unhappiness. We are responsible for our own happiness and should not hang disappointment or discontentment on external events.

Your partner does not make you unhappy. He or she has no control over you. He or she does not *make* you anything. *It is you who are responsible for yourself.*

INTRODUCTION

It is a mistake to believe that we have to be loved by everybody.

It is a mistake to think it is wrong to be different.

As we begin to work, keep in mind that the purpose of counseling is not merely to *talk* about a problem. The purpose is rather to use active psychological tools to *resolve* a problem. The talk stage has one purpose—that of diagnosis. It serves to inform you as to why you are unhappy, to help you understand what is not right about your relationship, and to choose the right tools for change. The goal of this book is *action* and *change,* and the most important thing to remember is that *you can facilitate these changes yourself*. Remember the prerequisites we discussed above.

Many couples know they are not happy in their marriage, yet they don't have enough motivation or confidence to solve their problems. This book is designed to give you the tools and confidence to do exactly that.

Now, with the empty pages of your notebook waiting to receive your thoughts, you are ready to begin.

How to Be Your Own Marriage Counselor

1
The Myths about Marriage

Expectation

Has marriage become obsolete?

Increasing numbers of marriages fall apart each year; the rate of divorce spirals upward. Marriage, as an institution, certainly is on shaky ground. Yet, because we do not know of any other institution that can fulfill the same functions in society, it is worth examining the reasons why marriages break up. What is missing in the man-woman relationship? Generally, the missing ingredient is a *realistic concept* of intimate and lasting relationships.

For an institution that has existed for so long, there is surprisingly widespread ignorance about marriage. Married people are no better informed—just because they are involved in a marriage—than are single people. Older people are often as ignorant as young people. Even experience, the best teacher of many life subjects, fails to teach most men and women the difficult lessons necessary to make a marriage work. When two people consider marriage, they assume that they will be happy and fulfilled forever, simply because they choose to be married. They expect it to transform them, to expand their lives, to make the whole greater than the sum of the parts. This *can* happen, of course, but the ideal is difficult to achieve and requires great sensitivity and hard work by both partners.

A person who is about to marry expects to find another person who can fulfill and satisfy him or her completely. We take romance for granted, and assume that the romantic aspect of the man-woman relationship will automatically endure. We have great expectations about the quality and quantity of sexuality in a relationship. And we expect the marriage to last forever.

What a lot to ask, in an imperfect world full of imperfect people! Generally speaking, we have greater expectations than two people can satisfy for each other. And the more unrealistic the expectation, the more likely it is that the relationship will fail.

Unrealistic expectations work in a destructive manner. You start with a glowing picture of the future that is general, unspecific, vague, and perhaps even subconscious. Then you compare your actual life with your expectations. The result is disillusioning and can be disastrous. In a sense, then, *comparison* with an unreal model of marriage is really the thing that dulls, and eventually may kill, a relationship.

Is there another way to look at marriage?

Of course, there is. Our objective here is to present ways to counteract these unrealistic expectations. You will be able to examine your own expectations, understand them, and abandon those that are false—realizing that this is not what marriage is about. This process, although painful and difficult at times, has distinct advantages over another approach (actually a *retreat*) which is most commonly used. Many people simply move out of one relationship into another, and often carry with them the same set of unrealistic expectations. Thus, there is the same probability that disillusionment will carry forward into the new relationship, and still another.

Expectations are built on myth. That is why they are complex and difficult to change. Every person subscribes to many myths, the elusive wisps of dream and imagination that are part of our human makeup. While myths and expectations are wonderful creations of the human mind, they can also portray an idealistic objective which is realistically impossible to achieve. And when the person does not achieve his or her expectation, or when reality pales compared to the myth, the consequences are usually destructive.

Mythical Expectations

An important distinction must be drawn between expectations based on role concepts, and those based on myths. Much popular literature on the changing styles of marriage now focuses on roles: who will earn the money, who will make the beds, who will diaper the baby, who will mow the lawn. Discussion and definition of roles before marriage is healthy and beneficial, but the hidden "time bomb" remains if myths aren't explored and brought into focus. Even the man and woman who enter a marriage with total agreement about the roles of husband and wife can still harbor unreal expectations. These are most often rooted in the following myths:

Myth #1: Love will conquer all.

Love will continue without any attempts to nourish it. Love is magically present or tragically absent. Attempts to "construct" love are cold, mechanistic, lacking in spontaneity, and therefore somehow inappropriate.

Here is an example of this myth, which holds that it is enough to be in love and that everything else will automatically fall into place in the relationship if you only possess that one key.

Judy has been married for more than a year. She is unhappy. During most of the time they have been married, her husband has not talked about his feelings for her. He comes home tired, checks the mail, reads the paper, and gets ready for dinner. She is waiting for a sign of personal praise or recognition, but receives none. She tries to draw him out with positive comments but he does not respond. So Judy has decided it's no use and has withdrawn into herself, disillusioned and disappointed.

In this case, Judy made the mistake of assuming that the ardor of premarital love would continue into the marriage, lifting them as a couple above the commonplace problems of the world. Her husband, David, made the false assumption that his wife would know, without being told, that his love was strong and enduring. As he went about his work, which he considered an expression of his love, he did not understand that the strength of love comes from continued constructive actions by both parties.

Love does not conquer all other needs. Judy needs to know that David loves her, to be *told* now and then that what she is doing pleases, or displeases, him. She also needs reaffirmation that other aspects of their lives are fulfilled, and that David comes home because he is happy to be with her and to talk to her.

Love—like any other living thing—must be nourished. A vital relationship requires constant attention, dedication, and work. Effort devoted to a relationship brings many rewards, if it is *mutual* effort. Perhaps because of their social conditioning, women are more likely than men to acknowledge that they must "make an effort" to keep the relationship alive. However, this effort is often directed toward personal appearance alone. Or toward being the "good wife"—that is, living up to a stereotype. Neither of these efforts really comes to grips with the need to nourish the *interaction* between husband and wife as unique individuals.

The husband must also contribute. Many husbands may realize the necessity for this, but lack the skills to do it. Traditionally, men neglect this area because social stereotypes have implied that it is primarily the woman's obligation to adapt to her husband's needs. Preoccupation with romantic interaction has typically been a feminine trait. While love cannot be created simply by an act of will, some ingredients of love—respect, friendship, companionship, nurturing, communication, helping, and excitement—can be cultivated. And love does not exist as an entity unto itself. Partners must each make a daily *decision* to love, if love is to continue.

Myth #2: Sexual attraction will continue at a high level of intensity.

Sex will be fantastic all the time. If sex isn't excellent at first, it will become so through practice. In a good marriage sex is super all the time.

The great amount of attention devoted to sexual matters in recent years has resulted in deep concern over the frequency of sexual intercourse. Many couples fear their marriage is "sliding downhill" if sexual relations occur less frequently as the years pass. This can result in a sense of obligation to keep up the pace in order to maintain a good marriage, and sex becomes a chore, making matters worse.

One couple I've counseled has been married for fifteen years. Helen, who always has been motivated to "satisfy" her husband, was concerned that she and John were not making love as frequently as in the early years of marriage.

More and more often, John was tired or failed to maintain an erection during intercourse. Helen worried that he no longer loved her.

After I encouraged them to examine and discuss the situation together, both came to realize that they had fallen into routine patterns of love-making and that John's capacity for sexual intercourse would naturally decline with age. I also encouraged this couple to experiment with different techniques of love-making, and to stress *quality* of *loving,* rather than *frequency* of love-*making.* They found new depths of enjoyment in each other, especially when John was reassured that it was not always necessary for him to "produce on demand."

Sexual anxiety also results from current myths about how a woman must respond or what a man must produce. The game becomes one of counting climaxes or measuring erections. A woman who does not reach climax may fake it, an act which diminishes her own honest enjoyment of sexual tenderness. Or, she may blame her husband for not "giving her" a climax. Or the man may blame her. Because achieving climaxes has become the be-all and end-all of sexual contact, anxiety results. This anxiety leads to finding fault with a partner. Once one starts blaming the other for the absence of a woman's climax or the insufficiency of the man's erection, the marriage is headed for trouble.

Myth #3: You can keep the "spark" in your marriage forever.

Only those who don't love each other any more lose the spark. If the spark is gone, your marriage is dead.

When people talk of keeping or losing the spark, they are referring to the original attraction which drew them together. The spark is one of those vague ingredients of mythical expectation. Marriage is seldom as exciting as the first date. It cannot always retain the igniting spark because infatuation, the specific compulsion and excitement of a new relationship, is based on the thrill of discovery, of meeting a stranger and coming to know a person.

Many people want to know how to bring back the spark into their marriage. They are disappointed when they learn, realistically that this can't be done. Once you know a person intimately, you can't retain the thrill of newness and discovery. It is a contradiction in terms. Once you have lived together for five, ten, or twenty years, you cannot retrieve the experience of first living together. Moments, and years, pass. If you must have the continuous excitement of new love, the only way to find it is to move from one relationship into another. You cannot have both a life of "new love" and a lasting, intimate relationship; you must choose one or the other.

However, you need not give up the possibilities of a rewarding marriage when you relinquish your craving for the original spark. You can find or create new excitement. You can savor each portion, each new phase, of your life together.

In parenthood, for example, you start something new, unknown, and creative. When you move to a new house or city, you have a new life to carve out together. When your children leave home, you have an opportunity to experiment with life styles, travel, new freedom together. If you seize each moment in a long, well-known relationship, and bring to it the joint creation of something new, you will find that you have no cause to mourn the inevitable passing of the spark that lit the fire in the first place.

Myth #4: A good marriage is totally harmonious.

You are never justified in disagreeing with your partner. Your partner is never justified in disagreeing with you.

Human relationships as intimate and intense as marriage can never be totally harmonious. Yet, many marriages pictured by Hollywood, on television, or in children's books are sweet, loving, and free of conflict. Naturally, children pick up the idea from these sources that the "normal" marriage is uniformly harmonious. Some children may temper this picture with their own family experience, or they may have trouble reconciling the two views.

If a family is reasonably happy, the child has a model against which to compare fiction. However, most children do not come from happy homes. The divorce rate is one proof of this; and if we are to assume that many parents stay together only "for the sake of the children," we can conclude that many newlyweds today were children in an unhappy family only yesterday. Unhappy homes make children insecure and unhappy. The child in such a home is likely to vow to himself that his own marriage will be different. The child vows that *his* marriage will be happy; *he* will avoid the mistakes of his parents; *he* will love without ever hurting; *he* will make his partner happy, and his partner will make him happy.

In making these vows, the child commits himself to the impossible. Since he has no model of a real-life happy family, he constructs the fantasy of a happy family in his mind. Later, when he or she marries, the wonderful intentions are all geared to achieve the impossible. A person becomes hurt, angry, and disappointed when the reality of marriage does not measure up to the myth-fed fantasy. A person then may feel "obligated" to get a divorce, reasoning that to remain in a disappointing marriage would be to admit that he could not do better than his parents.

It is far better to understand that happiness does not imply or require perfection. Nor is it necessary to squelch negative feelings. One cannot always avoid hurting a partner. Feelings that are bottled up—whether negative *or* positive—create tension that is potentially explosive in a marriage.

The Myths about Marriage

Myth #5: Fighting is irrational.

There are solutions to all problems if you are only calm and rational about things. A person who is irrational is wrong. Don't ever disagree.

This commitment to rationality runs afoul of reality very quickly. Sometimes there are no rational reasons for the motivations, preferences, desires, and feelings that come into conflict. Human beings don't always have reasons for the way they behave. What may seem trivial to you may be important to your spouse. Your values may simply be different. Your spouse might lose his patience and explode about things that in your mind are insignificant or stupid. There's the classic example of the mate who insists on squeezing the toothpaste from the middle of the tube. One might become annoyed because the other leaves shoes by the side of the bed. (The mate doesn't see anything wrong with this, since the shoes will be put on again the next morning!)

Some couples never get over this stage of the relationship. The world is full of couples who, after twenty years of marriage, are spitefully arguing and, when they are not arguing, are carrying a load of feelings of irritation, hostility, and resentment.

Couples cannot expect rational solutions to all of their conflicts. The differences between two people are usually based upon different emotional responses to a situation. You can't ignore those differences simply because they are irrational, and you cannot eliminate them by trying to reason with each other.

Everyone is irrational about some preferences and dislikes in life. Often habits are acquired from childhood behavior that was approved by parents. An adult, so conditioned, then derives a sense of comfort from doing things in a certain way, and his or her way of doing things may well be irrational. Thus, no one in a marriage is "right" or "wrong," and conflict is not resolved by proving one is right and the other wrong.

Being calm and reasonable in decision-making is often important. But learning to fight is also important, and is necessary to resolve many conflicts. Solutions to some problems will come only through fighting.

Fights, of course, should be strictly limited to the immediate issues at hand, and not used as a dumping ground—by either partner—for all the other irritations that may have accumulated over the years of a marriage. Fight about one thing at a time, and force yourselves to *agree* on the limits before you start. Surprisingly, such an agreement often eliminates the need to fight in the first place. I discuss how to fight fairly later in the book.

Myth #6: Your marriage should be "normal."

Many couples confronting marital difficulties seek a solution by asking: "What is normal?"

Unfortunately, there is no objective measure of a "normal" marriage. In fact, if we look for an *average* marriage, the divorce rate is evidence that the average marriage is unhappy.

The best thing is to forget about external standards. Focus on your own priorities and values. The amount of conflict or communication that is right for your relationship is whatever makes you feel comfortable. YOU. Not a stereotyped image which you believe should be your yardstick.

Although we cannot discuss a normal marriage, we *can* set for ourselves the goal of a *healthy* marriage. A healthy relationship is one in which two people level with each other. In a healthy relationship, the partners deal with each other as equals rather than attempt to manipulate each other, dominate, or play games. A healthy relationship is based upon openness and trust.

Myth #7: Marriage will remove your feelings of worthlessness.

You will find compensation for the lack of love in your earlier life.

This is a forlorn hope, because it can never be completely fulfilled. And, if you subsequently blame your partner—or your marriage—for your unfulfilled hopes, you are on the road to disaster.

Many people have suffered a painful lack of love from parents in childhood. Love deprivation causes insecurity and yearning for an all-encompassing, unconditional love which will fill the emptiness. This is a longing for *parental* love, and a marriage partner can never give you something missing from years ago, because those years have passed. No matter how much a person now loves you, he or she cannot erase years of longing. You will always feel like the child who was unloved by your parents. You cannot change the fact that they did not love you, or did not express their love clearly to you.

The task in marriage is to focus on what you have *now*. Focusing on adult love will at least help to dissolve a continuing sense of suffering. Don't ask your spouse to be the parent to a child who suffered long ago; ask him to love the person who exists now.

If you suffer from feelings of worthlessness or self-hate, your self-esteem is low. If your feeling of worthlessness is strong, do not expect your partner's love to automatically supply you with a feeling of self-worth. Love can ease the pain and help you to find the courage to work through your own problems. It does not deliver absolute self-esteem and happiness. You must save yourself.

Some young men and women marry at an early age to escape their parents and an unhappy family situation. Such marriages often fail. Here we find a person, or both persons, desperately hoping that marriage will be the solution to unhappiness. There is no assurance that it will be. Such a marriage is especially problem-filled when the unhappy person has low self-esteem, and therefore chooses a partner who is really unsuitable. This commonly happens because an individual's low self-esteem causes him to feel, "I don't deserve better." Thus, a sensitive and intelligent man might marry a coarse and dull woman, or vice versa. They are mismatched from the beginning, and so their relationship can never be one of full sharing and growth. In fact, if this man comes to a point later in life where his self-esteem improves, he finds himself in a situation where he must either reconcile himself to divorce, or live out life with an unsatisfying marriage.

In all marriages, we seek to move from myth to reality.

2
The Realities of Being Married

Marriage is *not* a myth. Marriage is not an answer to unfulfilled expectations. Marriage probably is not what you thought it would be.

What, then, is marriage, and what are the realities of being married?

Marriage is an expression of intimacy, security, companionship, and love. Marriage can, and should, be beautiful. It begins with two people falling in love and experiencing the wonderful feelings that they can share a life of love with each other. Unfortunately, problems often arise when romantic feelings collide with the daily realities of living together.

Obligations and Security

Sharing a life of love is what marriage can be. But one of the realities of marriage is that many people stay in a relationship when it is no longer satisfying. Why is this so?

Some people stay married out of a sense of obligation to their religion, to their children, or to their partner. Others remain in an unhappy situation because they have low self-esteem, which convinces them that they really don't deserve a better marriage than they have. Low self-esteem also fosters a feeling of hopelessness, a sense of despair over the possibility of improving life. This can manifest itself in overt cynicism, wherein the individual bitterly concludes that the reality of marriage is frustration, and it is therefore futile to exchange one relationship for another. This lack of self-esteem by one or both partners is a major cause of marital problems. It is important that each partner feel a healthy level of self-assurance before and during a relationship.

Individual needs are numerous and complex. One reason that two people enter a relationship is a desire for security. Conversely, many people stay in unsatisfying relationships because of insecurity, whether it be material, emotional, or intellectual. Let's examine each of these briefly.

Material Insecurity

At least until recent years, women were conditioned from childhood to see their role in life as wives and mothers. Few went to college to prepare for careers. As a result, they were afraid to consider being single and afraid of material insecurity. Obviously, then, when they entered a marriage, such women could not function as equal partners. Conflicts were generally resolved by feminine submission to the male point of view. Because of their material dependency, such women lost a measure of what was fair—their equal rights in a marital relationship. Eventually they even lost the capacity to realize the imbalance between the positive and negative aspects of their marriage. They came to accept everything as "normal."

Even today, when divorce is commonplace, insecurity is a common motive for a person to remain in an unhappy marriage, especially if there are children. Some women still feel insecure about their ability to support themselves, particularly if their education was interrupted by pregnancy and child-rearing. If such a woman pursues career training, once her children have left home or entered school, her insecurity over survival needs may be reduced. It is not surprising that many women terminate their unhappy marriages at this point.

Emotional Insecurity

Traditionally, women have also been more emotionally insecure than men. This is because until recently women were taught that their role in marriage was to be submissive and inferior to their husbands. Women were afraid to act or feel equal because it just was not part of the stereotyped role concept of the "positive wife." In a way, marriage gave women material security, while increasing their emotional insecurity!

The advent of the women's liberation movement is creating a positive change in the way many women perceive themselves. However, even the relatively liberated woman—and man—seems to be influenced in her or his choice of partner by the traditional tendency of women to marry men who are older, better educated, and perceived as being more intelligent than themselves. Many men still choose wives who are younger, shorter, less educated, and perceived as being less intelligent than themselves. (This tendency is generally used to explain why many intelligent and successful women are single—their male peers have chosen women "beneath" them.) The persistence of this mating gradient could perpetuate a tendency for women to feel inferior to their husbands—after all, they chose their man because they perceived him to be superior.

It is apparent, therefore, that as more women achieve better education and more equality in all areas of life, this aspect of emotional insecurity will be ameliorated. It has been my clinical observation that a woman who comes into a marriage with her own profession suffers less from both emotional and material insecurity. It seems that the knowledge that she *could* provide for herself if need be, and that she *chooses* her role freely in the relationship, enhances her sense of personal worth and independence.

Intellectual Insecurity

It is interesting that many women know that they are as intelligent or knowledgeable as their husbands, but regard this as their personal *secret!* The stereotype of a "good" wife has been that she does not disagree with her husband, certainly not in public. However, she should be challenging enough in her conversation to be *interesting to him*. The power of this expectation can be seen in husbands who are shocked, angered, or irritated if their wives disagree with their opinions on "intellectual" matters such as politics or economics. The man frequently assumes that his wife has made a total commitment to his intellect and his judgment.

Women, because of their social upbringing, frequently need to see the husband as the strong one—the rock of Gibralter, *their* strength. Even when a man is in fact a weak individual—insecure, neurotic, and unsure of himself— his wife may treat him like a king. Some women need to pretend to themselves that they have a strong husband, denying his weaknesses. Others attempt to help their man to be strong, because they see his weakness and are terrified. In either case, the relationship is brittle, and locked into a pattern of dishonesty.

So a fundamental reality of marriage is that it should not be based upon security needs, but rather upon equality, creativity, and intimacy.

Creative Marriage: Intimacy

In a creative marriage, an intimate relationship develops between two people who continue to grow, individually and as a pair.

You cannot relate to your partner intimately, or enjoy and appreciate his or her full intimate expression, if you don't like yourself. Liking yourself is where intimacy between two begins. It begins with the intimacy of one. By this I do not mean narcissism, but rather a realistic appreciation of your own self-worth.

Equality and *mutual commitment* are the keys to real intimacy with another person. *Connectedness* (the emotional feeling of specialness that exists between partners) plus *stability* and *permanence* are present in direct proportion to the feelings of mutual closeness and personal growth. You are *vulnerable* when you expose your weaknesses and your needs to another person. You are *exclusive* when you are not willing to share your intimate needs with your partner or anyone else.

Each person needs to know that he or she is the most important, the most special friend of the partner. Both have established their highest priority as being *with* and *for* each other. Also their availability to each other is higher, and takes precedence over availability to anyone else. Intimacy is a *choice,* and intimacy between partners is subject to vulnerability to, and rejection by, the other.

Partnership through Choice

The concept of choice is essential to the realities of marriage. The commitment starts with the choice two people make to be together, the choice of a partner who is to become the most significant associate in life.

Commitment is a free choice that *each person continues to make throughout the marriage*. At the same time, husband and wife both enjoy the freedom of individual feelings and the expression of those feelings, whether positive or negative. That is, the freedom to be *you*.

If you recognize that the commitment to marriage is *always* a commitment by choice, you are also ready to see marriage as a union of *equals*. Equality is one of the essential realities in a successful, creative marriage. Equals take risks in being honest with each other, in expressing the need to feel secure. Expressing such needs also makes you vulnerable if you are dependent for emotional or material survival upon your partner. Yet it is the willingness to take this risk that leads to genuine intimacy.

Equals have the strength to assert themselves, to express disagreements, to fully experience their humanness—and to ask for help. For a marriage in which two equals feel free to continue growing separately as well as together, *trust* in one's self and one's partner is essential.

Now, let's look at some of the other realities of marriage. (For further discussion of the realities of marriage, refer to *Changing Your Lifestyle* by Frieda Porat, Ph.D., and Karen Myers.)

Reality #1: We are not in love all the time.

We move into and out of a relationship in a certain rhythm, and the rhythm is ours. At times we feel very close, loving, and intimate, but a short time later we can feel contented although separate and distant from our partner. This does not mean that we stop caring and loving; it only means that the relationship changes in intensity as the moods of the partners change. This is a normal and natural fluctuation.

Give yourself permission *not* to feel that you must be close all the time, not to feel obligated, and not to feel that it is a duty to love. These self-imposed demands can destroy the freedom to be yourself. You—with mood swings, ups and downs—and your partner with his or her individual pace, will flow toward and away from one another within a healthy relationship.

Reality # 2: We cannot fulfill all the needs of our partner.

In an intimate relationship, each of us is limited in our ability to fulfill what our partner needs in life. You are not the mirror image of the person you marry. Two people never have exactly the same interests or capacities. Respect your partner for what he is, see him for *who* he is rather than trying to change him. We are all different. Accepting and respecting the differences between yourself and your partner is the only way a marriage can continue.

Consider the wide range of human needs—intellectual, professional, emotional, spiritual, and physical. To expect one person to provide stimulation and satisfaction in all these areas is unrealistic and futile. One partner, for example, might need intellectual discussion in areas where the spouse is ignorant or uninterested. It is important to look for the fulfillment of such a need within oneself or in other resources, such as friends, lectures, books, or classes, rather than to view the partner as inadequate or inferior.

A person may have emotional needs which the partner either cannot, or chooses not to, fulfill. A wife, as an example, may need a listener, someone to listen to an expression of feelings pent up over a long period of time. If the partner is not happy or comfortable in the role of listener, he is justified in declining to hear her out. There are other ways to deal with and to express feelings. Share them with a friend, for example, or express them in a group encounter. Write them down in a journal, or express them in other art forms.

Many couples do not share the same interest in sports or other physical activities, such as dancing, hiking, or swimming. You can each fulfill your own needs alone or join a club or class to find people with whom to share these activities. Again, don't expect your partner to share naturally all of the physical activities that interest you.

A special physical need is sexual expression, which evokes exceptional rules and commitments in marriage. Unless *both* partners choose a marriage style wherein sex is not exclusive with the marriage partner, sex will be an expression of total intimacy which cannot include others. For this reason, sexual activity and communication require special nurturing. Both partners must be committed to their sexual evolution as a couple. Sexual interrelation is both intense and troublesome for many couples. The topic will be discussed more thoroughly in a separate chapter.

Reality #3: Most disagreements and differences between partners can be resolved through compromise.

Most disagreements do not stem from one person being right and the other wrong. The goal, then, is to find a solution that two people can accept and which allows them to live comfortably without sacrificing or changing themselves to the point where they resent the relationship. Many issues are trivial. And many marriages break up because of the inability to compromise on trivia.

Here are some of the trivial complaints I have heard shouted by two people, just before divorce:

"Why don't you keep your clothes more tidy?"

"Why are you always late?"

"Why is dinner never ready on time?"

"Why am I always the one to give in?" (Or "to plan the weekend?" or "to take out the garbage?")

The list of such minor, but irritating, complaints is endless, and here is where you can begin using your notebook. Write down a list of small things your partner does regularly that irritate you. Then exchange lists with him or her. You may be surprised—and even amused—when you express your feelings by writing the list and then by reading the things that irritate your spouse. Bringing such things out into the open can help to relieve the sting.

The art of marriage depends upon the ability to say, "You do it this way, I do it my way. Let's find a solution in which both of us can continue living together without being annoyed with each other about these issues." Here is the essence of a workable compromise and you will have the opportunity, by working with this book, to practice the art of compromise.

As you see, disagreeing about trivial matters is common in marriage. Paradoxically, most couples cope much better with the big issues in their lives, such as moving to a new house, caring for a sick child, or changing jobs. Repeated small irritations are the ones that most generally cause you to lose your patience.

Now, let's move a step beyond the lists of trivia that you wrote down a short time ago. Try the following exercise:

First, write down in your notebook your irritations and arguments about trivial matters in a week's time, like the following examples:

Day	Content	Spouse's Response
Saturday, 11/4	I left my clothes on the floor.	You are like having another baby around the house. Can't you ever pick up after yourself?
Sunday, 11/5	I lounged around the house in my underwear.	Why do you have to be such a slob? What if company came and found you like that?
Monday, 11/6	I came home late from work.	I can't trust you. You never keep track of time.

Second, after you have written a weekly summary of what irritated your spouse and what he or she said, try *reversing roles* and imagine being the partner who reacts to these trivial incidents. Assume that your partner left his clothes in the living room, or wandered around the house on Sundays with her hair up in curlers. What would you say and do? Suppose your wife came home an hour late when she was supposed to meet you for a date. How would you feel and what would you say?

Third, hold a dialogue with your partner, discussing your feelings about your list of trivia. She will then share her list of trivia with you.

Fourth, rethink and change your attitude. This may seem to be a large order all at once, but what it suggests is to find a new perspective about these trivial irritations and to arrive at some workable solution.

You will read more about how to negotiate disagreements constructively in a later chapter, but the first step—as revealed to you by this exercise—is to become aware of the minor irritations which damage your relationship. Then, since most such minor irritants involve careless habit, you can focus on making the minor changes which will please your partner, or let him or her know why you are not willing to change. Further, solving minor problems through compromise teaches you to deal with major conflicts.

Reality #4: We are not perfect.

No one is perfect. We are neither entirely strong nor totally weak, all giving nor all taking. We are all of these things at different times to varying degrees. Learning to accept the range of qualities in a partner, and not to make judgments about that person, is to acknowledge the existence of a real person, and not a stereotype or model.

Each person has many positive qualities to offer, qualities that most likely accounted for the initial attraction between partners. Each of us can choose to focus on the positive elements we give to and receive from each other, the pleasures we get and give, and at the same time to accept the shortcomings of the other. After all, to see a fault in a partner involves a subjective judgment on your part. If your partner feels comfortable in the ways she does things, the ways in which she functions and relates to you, learn to accept the person as she is.

Can You Live with the Realities?

No one but you can decide if you will be able to live with the realities of being married. You must decide that for yourself. You must look at the advantages and disadvantages to *you* of being married. And you must look at the advantages and disadvantages of being single. You must look at the investment that is necessary to make a marriage work and decide whether or not the investment will pay off for you.

Here is a brief checklist to help you decide if you can live with the realities of being married. Answer "yes" or "no" to each of the questions, even if you are now married and have been for some time.

Are You Willing to Learn New Skills?

It takes certain skills to keep a relationship alive. If you want a beautiful garden, you have to develop gardening skills. You must learn about soil and watering and fertilizer. Starting with beautiful, healthy plants is only the beginning. If you fail to nourish them, they will never bloom.

You can learn the skills to nourish a relationship just as you can learn other skills. But the skills used in creating a healthy marriage are generally not taught in our families or in our schools. You can hardly be blamed for being a novice in these skills, but you *can* be blamed for not learning them. Reading this book, in fact, indicates that you are willing and able to learn and use new skills.

Are You Willing to Continue Working?

Both partners must be willing not only to learn the skills necessary for creating a deep, lasting, and intimate relationship, but also to work at it as long as you remain together. Some people say, "We've worked so hard for a year (or a month), can't we relax now?" The answer is, "No," you can never relax completely. The effort and attention required to maintain a happy marriage must become second nature all of the time. Just as you breathe, eat, and sleep every day to maintain life, so you must practice every day the skills of communication, intimacy, sex, and expressing anger to keep your marriage alive.

Are You Willing to Be Honest?

Can you be more honest with yourself? This means openly facing your strengths and weaknesses, the things you like about yourself and the things you would like to ignore. Can you accept the bitchy, angry parts of yourself as well as the sweet and loving qualities? Can you feel good about expressing honestly the full range of your thoughts and feelings?

Next, are you willing to be honest with your partner? Are you willing to let him or her see the things you are ashamed of, as well as the things you are proud of? Can you express the negative feelings as well as the positive feelings? Do you want to? The expression of negative feelings and the fluctuation in feelings is an important part of the marriage relationship.

Being honest is difficult, because in doing so a person must take risks and become vulnerable. Any time you express an honest need, a deep feeling, you risk rejection. Yet when both partners are capable of communicating and saying, "I feel low, I need you, I need help," or "I feel angry," they are paving the way for a healthy relationship.

In a healthy marriage, both partners accept the fact that individual moods change and that the mood of the relationship changes. Thus, an expression of anger or need can be made without threatening your mate.

Are You Willing to Participate in Conflict?

Conflicts never cease to occur in a marriage because two people are always different and their differences will emerge if they are being honest. You must express your feelings and your needs and allow your partner to do the same. And when feelings and ideas come into conflict, they can be resolved in a way that is satisfying to both partners.

A word of caution here, however: while negative feelings and conflict resolution should be a part of marriage, some couples fall into an excessively negative pattern in which it is easier to complain than to praise. The negative input far outweighs the positive input. Eventually, in this kind of situation, neither partner listens to the other because the complaints recur like lyrics on a broken record.

Furthermore, there are limits to negative expression. Honesty and authenticity never imply a license for cruelty or insensitivity. When negative feelings are expressed as a step toward building a successful relationship, they can and should be expressed in a way that does not damage your partner.

When negative feelings have been expressed, and the partners listen openly to each other, conflicts will be more clearly understood by both. The next step is to work on solutions that will satisfy both partners and contribute to a harmonious relationship.

Are You Willing to Give Up Old Scripts?

Most of us reach adulthood behaving according to unwritten scripts from our past, scripts related to the myths that haunt us. These scripts include a vision of the "good wife" and the "good husband." Uncovering unrealistic scripts takes time and development of new insights. *Changing* the mental patterns requires hard work and new skills. Getting rid of the old scripts and learning new ways to develop as an individual and a couple, however, can be one of the most rewarding processes in life. It may be the only thing that will save your marriage.

If you answered "yes" to *any* of the questions above, you are ready to begin accepting the realities of being married. If you answered "yes" to *all* of the questions, you are ready to be your own marriage counselor. In any case, you are ready, with the help of this book, to acquire the skills which will make your marriage vital and rewarding both now and in the future.

The next step is to draw up and sign a mini-contract with your partner setting out the terms under which you are both willing to work.

The Mini-Contract

So you are not perfect and neither is your partner. Before you start learning the skills for maintaining a good marriage, you need to make a joint decision and an agreement to work at it sincerely *for at least three months*. This is the first mini-contract between you and your partner. It must include the following elements:

1. You will put time aside—*prime* and *committed* time—to work alone and with your partner, twice a week, for one to two hours at a time.
2. You will work with your partner and spend fifteen minutes each day answering the questions at the end of the chapters in this book. After you answer the questions alone, you will then share your answers with your partner.
3. At this point, you *rethink*—that is, change your attitude, and practice the new attitude. Remember to praise your partner as he or she is trying to make changes in behavior. A word of praise can go a long way, especially in trying to encourage *new* behavior.
4. After you come to a workable conclusion, then move on to the next chapter of the book.

You may decide the speed of your own program, and some chapters of the book will require more attention than others, but I would recommend spending about a week per chapter. This will set out for you a ten- to twelve-week program which corresponds roughly to the term of your first mini-contract. If you both agree to learn and practice the skills covered in the chapters to come, I am confident that you will enrich your marriage without the help of a professional counselor in private sessions.

Remember to use your notebook at all times—not only for the questions and answers, but to jot down ideas, new insights, and feelings which come to you as you work together. Divide the notebook into sections according to book chapters, and then devise whatever work system feels comfortable.

Mini-Contract Sample

I, _____, promise I am willing to devote the necessary time and energy to explore my relationship with _____ _____, my partner.

I am willing to:
  learn new skills,
  practice new skills,
  continue a maintenance program,
  spend two hours per week with my partner going over material in this book.

I am also willing to be:
  honest,
  open,
  nonattacking,
  nondefensive,
  a participant in conflict resolution.

The Realities of Being Married

I am willing to give up old:
   outdated scripts,
   false expectations,
   ineffective habits,
   stereotypic ways of thinking,
   destructive behavior.

I am ready to learn new:
   scripts,
   realistic expectations,
   attitudes,
   positive thoughts,
   constructive behavior.

Signed _____

_____

Date _____

Witnessed by _____
(a friend)

Now you are ready to begin. With a positive attitude, you will achieve what you want.

Merging Myths and Realities

Remember, one of the most important things we are trying to do at this point is help you to step away from the myths from your past, and to create new realities for yourself and your partner. Although the process is simple, most people must invest considerable time and patience to make the required changes. Briefly, these are the steps you will go through.

1. *Recognize your own unrealistic expectations.* Do you expect your wife to be always charming, beautiful, and well-groomed despite the work she has been doing throughout the day? Do you expect your husband to be always strong, wise, understanding, and protective? Do you expect your sex life to be always perfect? These are just a few of the possibilities.

2. *Identify what your partner is capable of changing and willing to change.* Does your wife clutter the bathroom with laundered nylons? Does your husband leave tools strewn around the garage floor and driveway? Start with the small ones and work up to the big ones.

3. *Identify the areas that you are not willing to change or are not capable of changing.* Does your husband drink so much that it worries you? Does your wife eat too heavily, gaining weight as she compensates for other frustrations? Do you both stubbornly insist that you deserve such small pleasures from life?

4. *Work out compromises that are agreeable to each partner.*

Do *not* try to work on all irritating facets at once. Take one compromise at a time and the next one will be easier. Remember, as we work through the book chapter by chapter, you will be receiving additional guidance in each step. Following is an example of one couple's confusion about marriage myths and realities.

Bob and Meg came to me for marriage counseling. They had been married for five years and had a three-year-old daughter. Meg is a registered nurse. Bob is an internist in a large medical clinic. Meg expressed dissatisfaction with their relationship, and Bob indicated willingness to explore their problems.

I asked Bob what he wanted to get, for *himself,* from the counseling experience. He said he wanted to learn more about himself and about what was wrong in his relationship with Meg. He loved Meg and was unhappy because he didn't seem able to reach her.

I encouraged him to *ask* Meg what was missing in their marriage and why she was unhappy. It is amazing how many people, after months or years of marriage, simply do not tell each other their true feelings or ask just what they want. This often happens because they *believe* they understand each other, or because they hesitate to reveal their vulnerability by expressing a need.

Meg, in a composed and quiet voice, told Bob that he treated her the way his father had treated his mother—as if she were there just to serve him, and when she did not, he got angry. Bob was puzzled. He was not aware that he had treated his wife in this fashion. He believed that he had never expressed disappointment or irritation about the way she ran their home or prepared their meals.

It became clear, after a short discussion, that Meg held an image in her mind of what she should do as a wife who did not pursue her career. (She had made this decision herself after their daughter was born.) Although the image was unrealistic, she suffered discomfort and was hypersensitive to any sign of her husband's displeasure.

Their assignment for the next week was to clarify their role expectations for themselves and for their partner. These expectations were written down, examined, and discussed openly. When they met again with me, they both had come to realize that each wanted to do what he *thought* the other person wanted, rather than checking and understanding what the partner *really* wanted.

After this first enlightening experience, Bob and Meg learned to check things out honestly with each other, rather than assuming that they knew what the other person wanted and felt. This new arrangement obviously was more satisfactory to both of them.

You might ask yourself at this point why Meg and Bob had been unable to find the answers by themselves, without consulting a marriage counselor. In retrospect, the problem and its solution appear to be simple, but oddly enough, most people do not break through such a communications barrier until *given permission* to do so by a third party. In effect, I gave them permission to open their thoughts, needs, and feelings to each other. In this book, I likewise give you permission to break through whatever barriers are causing a breach, however large or small, between you.

An Exercise to Break Down the Myths of Marriage

Now you can begin to examine your own myths about marriage. Complete the following exercises.

A. Write down in your notebook all the statements you can think of about what you believe to be the perfect marriage. Then, in the columns to the right, write down the source of each notion, that is, *who* told you this is what a marriage should be. You may want to use your own format, or the following examples may be helpful.

Remember, these are only examples. You and your partner should feel free to add as many items to the list as you wish and to express them in any way, using as many words as are necessary to make the thoughts clear. Above all, try to precisely identify the source of your notions of what a marriage should be.

The Realities of Being Married

	Source		
The Perfect Marriage	**Parents**	**Self**	**Others**
1. I should _____			
2. He (she) should _____			
3. The house we have should			
4. The jobs we have should ___			
5. The income we have should			
6. The friends we have should			
7. Sex should be _____			
8. The feelings between wife and husband should be ___			
9. Marriage will bring _____			
10. After I have been married for a while _____			

B. Compose another list that *describes your reality*—how your marriage really is, not how you think it should be. For every item you wrote in part A, write a similar item describing how things really are.

C. Compose a third list that focuses on the aspects of your marriage that *dissatisfy* you now. What are the things you don't like in your partner? What don't you like in yourself? What would you like to change in your marriage?

Include trivia as well as the items you consider more important. As you undertake this exercise, consider that someone has given you permission to write down all the things that have been bothering you. Remember, you have already signed a mini-contract with your spouse to explore these areas with the understanding that you are not trying to hurt each other. To help you get started, here are some beginning phrases to start you expressing feelings, observations, and comments.

1. I don't like my partner's _____.
2. I don't like my _____.
3. If my partner would only _____.
4. If I could change five things about my partner, _____.
5. If I could change five things about myself, ____ _____.
6. The thing that bothers me most _____.
7. I wish he (she) would _____.
8. I wish I would _____.
9. I hate it when he (she) _____.
10. I hate it when I _____.
11. It bothers me when _____.

D. After you have completed the above lists (and be prepared that this may require several work sessions before you and your partner are finished with it), continue to write answers to the following questions in your workbook:

1. What were my expectations of marriage?
2. What did I expect from my partner?
3. What did I see as his (her) roles?
4. What personality did I hope he (she) would have?
5. How did I view love?
6. How did I feel about arguments, about fighting?
7. Did I feel our marriage would cure my hunger and need for self-esteem?
8. What choices have I made about our relationship in the marriage?
9. What are the commitments I made when we decided to get married?

The Realities of Being Married

As you can see, the previous lists and questions to answer represent work, but it is necessary work. The deeper you delve into your needs and feelings as you go along, the more beneficial this work will be.

After you finish writing, you'll probably heave a sigh of relief, but this is only the beginning.

Now trade lists with your partner. Once you have absorbed what he or she has written, discuss your lists point by point. As you discuss your own and your partner's myths and realities of marriage, the realities should emerge more clearly and you can begin to compromise and end the disparity between the two.

Perhaps you might even question whether your marriage style is right for you.

3
Marriage Styles

Have you ever stopped to think about your marriage style—the way you relate to your intimate partner, the way you live, the way you express your love?

Your marriage style is the composite of what you expect and receive from your partner, and from your life together. It is what you wish to accomplish together and the way you, as a couple, go about it.

Most people never realize that they are free to examine their existing marriage style, free to choose from several options, free to experiment with existing marriage styles, or to invent a new and different one to suit their own needs.

Many couples are stuck in a certain way of relating to each other and living together, just because their parents and grandparents and all their relatives lived that way. They conclude, "This is the way to be and act when you get married." Often, after a few years of living together, they feel stifled, bored, stale, and they reach another conclusion. "My partner is boring, unfulfilling, and stifling; therefore, I

Marriage Styles

have to dissolve this marriage and look for another partner."

What these people fail to understand is that most likely they will enter into *another* boring, unfulfilling, stifling marriage—only this time with a different partner. The question is, is it the way we go about the marriage that is so stifling, or is it the partner in *each* case, regardless of how many new partners there may be?

In most cases, the marriage style is at fault, and you are free to change that style. You may be reluctant to consider a different marriage style because you fear the unknown. Obviously, you don't know if something different would work for you. Perhaps you don't like experimenting. You might be more conservative and want to stick with what you've got.

This chapter describes various marriage styles which other people have chosen. None of them may be right for you, but considering the alternatives that are available to you may be the only realistic approach that will save and/or enhance your marriage.

If you choose to be married—and you wish to do everything you can to have a good, workable, rewarding, and happy marriage—then examining your marriage style and choosing with your partner the one that best fits *your needs today* is a good place to start.

Whether you have a problem in your marriage, or you want to learn skills to prevent future problems, or you have a good marriage that you would like to enrich, it's important to examine your options.

- What is your present marriage style?
- Would you like to develop a different style?
- What are the available marriage styles?

Here is a brief overview of various marriage styles as described in my book, *Changing Your Life Style:*

The "Fulfilled" Marriage

This marriage relationship fits all the conventional expectations for a marriage, but it is a myth because it is impossible. The myth of the *fulfilled* marriage presumes that two people can satisfy all the needs and expectations of the other, and by doing so they will be happy forever. The concept of the fulfilled marriage further implies that the very fact that each partner should and will be able to fulfill the other partner's needs makes for happiness. Paradoxically, it does not.

You may be shocked and disappointed by the notion that a fulfilled marriage is impossible because most people interpret this as being completely satisfied all of the time. If you consider this for a moment, you will realize that a constant state of satisfaction, or satiation, itself could become monotonous and therefore unsatisfying.

Be assured, there can be many *moments* of fulfillment within a marriage relationship, just as there are moments of excitement, humor, pain, and discontent. However, being fulfilled does not last. It is a momentary peak experience and people spend more time working toward moments of fulfillment, anticipating the richness of those moments, and then later savoring the memory, than they spend actually being fulfilled.

An obvious example is the sexual orgasm, which lasts only a few moments, but is accompanied by much longer periods of loving, caressing, and even anticipating the hour of making love. If we were able to live all of our lives in the midst of peak experience (which in essence is what we're talking about in the myth of the fulfilled marriage), then it would become monotony rather than peak experience.

A marriage in which each partner continually satisfied every need of the other—even if it were possible—would become stultifying. Still, some couples try for it. This type of marriage, based upon the myth of "two becoming one," is inhibiting, limiting, enforced togetherness. It is marked by fixed and rigid role assignments. Each partner possesses the other and this exclusive "ownership" limits each partner's development. The fulfilled traditional marriage often sets up an unequal status between man and woman with the woman coming out on the short end. There is a lack of personal freedom which eventually leads to boredom because stimuli from the outside are shut out or limited.

If we see our life within a marriage as a complete world of *you* and *me,* then *us* is the union. In a fulfilled marriage, the union looks like this:

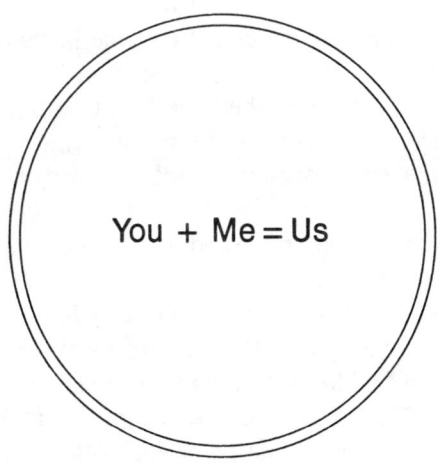

The two circles of *you* as an entity and *me* as an entity overlay each other completely. In this togetherness (another word, like fulfilled, which sounds good at first) there is no room for reaching out, for admitting that there are times and places when and where you need separateness. Neither partner acknowledges the freedom to disagree, to be sad, to be you. You may be stifled, swallowed, and drowned by this togetherness. In a fulfilled marriage you:

1. deny your right to be yourself;
2. own and possess each other;
3. live a life of pretense that you are a quasi-god to each other, and as such you have the ability to fulfill *all* of each other's needs *all* of the time;
4. don't question your roles because that's the way it was and that's the way it will remain.

Fulfilled marriage offers the illusion of security, but it stunts the growth of individuals. In this type of marriage, your dependency upon each other is created by manipulation. The husband in a fulfilled marriage depends upon his wife to provide all the traditional feminine services (creature comforts); the wife depends upon the husband to give her security, and to make her feel needed. The woman is expected to be passive and obedient (the traditional female role), while the man is expected to be authoritarian and controlling (the traditional male role). Even in the most loving and tender relationships, these stereotyped roles and their interaction between man and woman can lead to utter boredom and frustration.

I counseled one married couple who had set as their goal the task of being totally aware of each other's needs and being committed to satisfying those needs.

Carl and Tina were sensitive people, actually hypersensitive to the wishes and needs of each other. In the early years, this seemed to be a perfect marriage in which both husband and wife gave up pieces of their own individuality in order to please the other. They tried to mind-read each other, often assuming that a momentary depression or feeling of worthlessness for one was the other's fault.

In later years, when Carl and Tina finally learned from long experimentation that neither could *make* the other happy all of the time, their marriage almost toppled to the opposite extreme in which the two ignored the other's needs. Thus, their earlier state of hypersensitivity to each other evolved into a steady state of dull unhappiness. By trying to fulfill each other totally, neither was fulfilled as an individual.

The Limited Partnership

Another option in marriage is the *limited partnership*.

Are you becoming confused by the word partnership? Does the word sound too businesslike, cold, and impersonal for application to a marriage? Let's look at what we mean by a partnership.

A partnership can be defined as a commitment between interested parties to join together in a venture in which everyone gains. A business partnership is set up primarily for monetary gain. In a marriage partnership, the gain may be partially material, but emotional as well. The more effective the partnership, the more gain both parties will receive; therefore, the more incentive they will have to stay in it and renew it.

If the gains are unlimited, why do we define this category of marriage as a limited partnership?

The nature of the limited partnership is that both partners *realize* and *accept* the fact that their partner has limitations. They also recognize that they have limited power to change each other. If your partner chooses to change, it will be because of his or her own free will, and not because of coercion on your part. Each partner is totally responsible for his or her own changes. You cannot make the changes for someone else. Each person must choose his own.

In a limited partnership, a man and woman enter the marriage as *equals*. The strength in such a relationship is that you stay in it because *that is your desire,* because you feel that enough of your high priority needs are being met to make the relationship worthwhile.

How do couples who are living in a limited partnership deal with the question of sexual attraction and activity with *others outside* of the marriage? Here is an isolated example of what we mean by partners approaching as equals and agreeing upon a style of marriage. Some of the options such a couple could consider are:

Option #1: The partners may agree to be completely monogamous. They can agree to friendships outside the marriage with a member of the opposite sex, but no sexual relations with that person.

Option #2: Both partners may agree to complete sexual freedom outside of the marriage, without sharing the details with each other.

Option #3: Both partners may agree to total sexual freedom outside of the marriage and complete sharing of these experiences with each other. This option seems the hardest to live by for any extended period of time. As the O'Neals say in *Open Marriage,* "Jealousy rears up in all but the rare man or woman whose self-confidence permits hearing about the partner's extramarital affairs without feeling some threat."

In the three options just described, the same rules apply to *both* partners. Both agree to what each partner wants.

But what if they do not agree? What if one partner wishes to remain monogamous while the other wants sexual relations outside the marriage? Here, again, are some of the options:

Option #1: The partner who wishes to remain monogamous can agree to the other partner being nonmonogamous as long as he is discreet and does not share these experiences with the other. The man and woman here accept the fact that they do not have the right to impose their values upon each other. There is room for dissension. The partners do not have to lie, and can avoid guilt feelings. The overall attitude between these partners is that of compromise and self-control.

Option #2: The partners may not be willing to work out a compromise. One solution, then, is to dissolve the marriage. Another is to hide your outside relations and not tell your partner the truth. In this situation, the partner having the affair must fully understand the risk he or she is taking by breaking the commitment of monogamy with the partner who does not wish to reach a compromise.

Unwillingness to compromise pushes your partner into a corner. You force him to take a drastic step which is not really his first choice. He must dissolve the marriage because he does not want to lie, or he must lie because he does not want to dissolve the marriage. If he lies, he does not like himself, and he does not like you for forcing him to be in such a position. Furthermore, he does not fully enjoy his outside experience because of the resentment and guilt he's feeling about being a liar without really wanting to be.

If he dissolves the marriage he is punishing himself because he really wants to continue the marriage. He is also punishing you and the children you may have. Everyone loses.

Option #3: The partner who desires an outside affair may decide not to pursue it in order to save the marriage. That decision may well cause him or her to resent the partner who would not compromise on the question of extramarital sex, and that resentment itself may prove toxic to the marriage relationship. That, in turn, may lead to eventual dissolution of the marriage, but at least the decision *not* to pursue the outside affair was a personal choice and therefore a legitimate part of the limited partnership.

At the same time, we should recognize that in many marriages, at some time, one or both of the partners may be drawn into a casual, unmeaningful, sexual relationship with another person. The marriage may survive, if the wandering member of the couple does not tell his partner, but this obviously is not the ideal way to behave when you have agreed to be open and considerate with each other on all issues.

Sexual relations are used here only as an example to show how the limited partnership can function to mutual advantage while respecting equality of individual rights and needs. Insofar as possible, avoid placing your partner in a bind—an impossible situation to which there is no workable solution.

Marriage Styles

Limited Partnership Advantages

The limited partnership presents numerous advantages over the fulfilled, or traditional, marriage. The limited partnership is:
- Realistic;
- Flexible;
- Exciting;
- Conducive to change and growth for both partners;
- Renewable and adaptable, it can accommodate the needs of both partners;
- Committed to the idea that both partners are equal.

A limited partnership allows for great freedom. Compare this with the fulfilled marriage, which provides very little freedom outside the marriage relationship.

We described the fulfilled marriage as a circle within a circle, with almost complete overlap. In the limited partnership, the amount of overlap between you and me is flexible and changeable. It allows for separateness, for individuality to express itself. A sizable portion of each circle always remains independent, self-sufficient and outside the relationship, as shown here.

As you can see from figure on the following page, the limited partnership allows each of you many freedoms to seek satisfaction of needs that cannot be fulfilled by your partner, areas of mutual independence from traditional husband/wife roles.

Perhaps, for example, you are a woman with important professional skills. The limited partnership should allow you full freedom to practice those skills without threatening the male partner (the traditional breadwinner). Both partners should be free to cultivate outside friendships.

A husband may be a movie fan while his wife prefers opera and ballet. Rather than each insisting the other take part in his or her preferred activities, each may go to the movies or opera alone, or find other friends with whom to share the experience.

There is a multitude of such examples, in which each person may wish to go his or her way from time to time. But the heart of the relationship lies in the couple's commitment to give their best time and energy to each other.

In a limited partnership, the separate portions can reach out in as many directions as necessary at any given time. Activities, friends, school, and so forth are always secondary to the relationship. The "quality time" or prime time, as shared *within* the marriage relationship, is of primary importance.

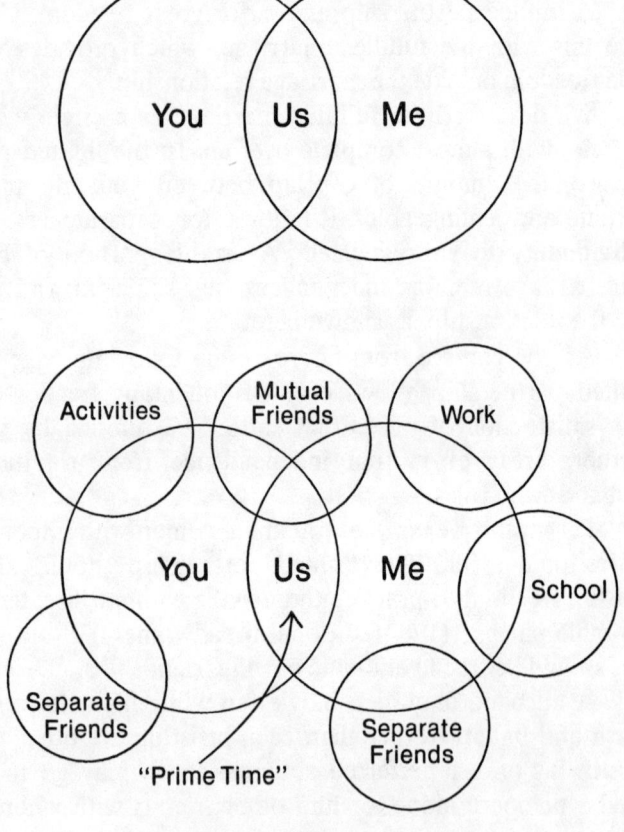

It is not a question of who has more activities outside the marriage. It is not a competition of winners and losers or a game of one upmanship. The extensions and the outside activities relate to the *needs* of each partner. Naturally, these needs vary from time to time. Limited partnership encourages the person to fulfill his needs. Some needs are fulfilled outside the marriage and some with the partner. Each person is nurtured in such a relationship.

The "Dead" Marriage

Sometimes the partners in a marriage are not relating in either a fulfilled style or a limited partnership style. They're not relating very much at all. This is often referred to as a dead marriage.

In this arrangement, the partners are superficially cordial, but distant. Their conversation focuses around trivia and they experience no quality time together. Their daily encounters are reduced to rituals. Their dialogue narrows to statements such as, "How are you?" or "Did you have a good day?" or "What are we having for dinner?" There is little intimacy between them. Their sexual relations are infrequent and mechanical. There is much submerged resentment, passivity, and unexpressed anger in this non-relationship relationship. The two people have resigned themselves to performing expected duties and leading a generally unfulfilled life.

Why do people remain in such a relationship?

Some are frightened of being alone. The unskilled, nonprofessional woman will stay in the marriage because of material dependency. She may accept her lot passively, or someday may try to change the relationship by seeking professional counsel. The man will often state that he is

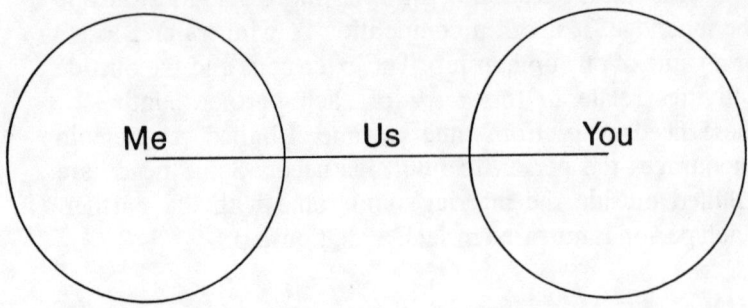

all right, that the problem rests with his wife, and that there is nothing wrong with the marriage.

You may ask yourself, "How can he be so unaware?" The issue may not be lack of awareness. Perhaps he feels genuinely satisfied with the marriage. Often, also, the man receives the extra strokes and recognition he needs from his job. The nonworking homemaker usually has no access to such emotional satisfaction.

What will happen to the dead marriage if both partners are not willing to revitalize it?

It will probably come to an end. The partners will not even experience a phase of mourning. The relationship may have been buried and the epitaph read many years ago.

Reasons for dissolving a dead marriage might be a new attachment outside the marriage for one of the partners, or completion of the parenting role when the last child leaves home. It often requires such a change or crisis for two people to recognize if their marriage has died or if it is possible to resurrect it.

Your Marriage Style Evaluation

Now that you have seen the different marriage styles—fulfilled marriage, limited partnership, and dead marriage—

Marriage Styles

it is time to take an inventory of your own marriage style. Here are some guiding questions. Answer "Okay" or "Not Okay" to each one.

1. Do you have meaningful contact with each other on a daily basis? (This means communication about needs, wishes, and desires, not just chit-chat.)
2. Do you have at least a weekly meaningful contact with each other?
3. Are you able to express your satisfactions and dissatisfactions to each other?
4. What are your expectations of your duties in the house?
5. Have you discussed your attraction to people of the opposite sex openly?
6. Do you feel that in your marriage sexual relations are discussed and agreed upon?
7. How do you feel about your partner's needs to have separate activities during the day, for example, continuing education, sports activities, involvement with friends, going away alone, or going away on vacation or a professional convention?
8. How do you feel about your needs to have separate activities during the day?
9. How do you feel about each of you having separate activities at night, such as school, sports, friends, or other such activities?
10. How do you feel about your partner having a friend of the opposite sex? How do you feel about them going out for lunch, going out in the evening, or going away for the weekend?
11. How do you feel about extramarital relations for your spouse?
12. How do you feel about extramarital relations for yourself?

Perhaps it is unnecessary to say that you and your partner must be careful to be totally honest with yourself and with each other in answering these and other questions posed throughout the book. After you have answered these —and your partner has done the same, *separately*—compare your feelings about your marriage style. Make notes in your workbook about your feelings and your partner's as you go along.

As to your marriage style, if you find that you are doing nearly everything together out of a sense of duty, and do not allow each other to pursue your own individual interests, then you have a *fulfilled* marriage in the sense described earlier in this chapter.

If, on the other hand, you spend prime time together while allowing your partner to pursue his or her own personal interests, then you have what we defined as a *limited partnership*.

And, if you find that you're not relating at all, you have a *dead* marriage. (Incidentally, if you and your partner were able to communicate with each other effectively in discussing the contents of this chapter, it's an initial indication that your marriage contains a spark of life after all.)

It should be made clear, also, that any marriage style is fine so long as both partners are satisfied and happy. We are not trying to dictate a way of life to you. You should lead the kind of life that is comfortable for *you*.

Now you've determined the type of marriage style you are leading. Are you happy with it? Do you want to make some changes? Are you both willing to work at it? Where do you go from here?

The next chapter supplies various questionnaires for a marital check-up that will help you determine which areas of your marriage need specific work. Remember to take a little bit at a time and use your workbook.

Do not try to make many major changes all at once.

If you try to change too much too quickly, you will not

Marriage Styles

be successful. More likely, you will throw up your hands in disgust and quit trying. Obviously, this does not lead to your original goal of trying to improve your marriage, which can be done only if you move gradually and methodically.

4
The Marital Check-Up

An annual visit to a doctor or dentist has become routine for most people who value their health and sense of well-being. The procedures are familiar from the moment you step into the doctor's office. You undress to allow him or her to examine you. You answer questions to reveal how each body system is functioning. Have there been any changes recently? Is there pain or discomfort? How are you eating and sleeping? How do you *feel?* The dentist or doctor then probes gently with the proper instruments, sometimes locating a tender area—a sign that a new problem may be developing. Finally, more extensive tests and X-rays are administered to reveal conditions that are not visible to the eye.

The same benefits we receive from medical and dental examinations can result from regular marital check-ups. You can conduct your own using this chapter as a guide, and every couple can benefit. Your purpose is similar to the medical examination—to uncover marital problems when they are small so that you may treat them before they reach a crisis that requires professional attention. On the other hand, you may conduct a check-up simply to verify that your marriage is in good health. In this case, the check-up is a technique for enriching your relationship and setting goals for future growth.

How do you react to the idea of conducting your own marital examination? Are you or your partner convinced that you need a check-up? If you feel shy about it, or unqualified, consider the next section carefully. Several common objections to the check-up are listed. Each is answered in a way that will help you get started. Various tables and questionnaires in this chapter are related to the work of George Bach and Peter Wyden in *The Intimate Enemy*.

1. *Why do we need a check-up for our marriage?*

The check-up is a positive, preventive process that can help every couple assess where they are today and where they want to be tomorrow. You can identify small problems and treat them before they mushroom into crises that threaten your marriage or require professional therapy. You can also use the check-up as a catalyst for the growth and enrichment of a relationship that is already healthy.

2. *I am happy with the way things are now.*

If you feel this way, use the check-up as a guarantee of continued happiness. Identify the things in your relationship that are successful, and build them into future plans. Have you discussed these with your wife or husband? Are both of you equally happy? The check-up is a good way to find out.

3. *If we probe into our marriage, it might start trouble.*

What will happen if you don't probe?

Will potential problems go away if they are hidden or ignored? It's far better to face the reality of your situation. And it is possible that if you examine your marriage, you may find it in better health than you think. However, if there are unsurfaced problems, wouldn't you rather find out now, when there is still time to correct them, than to find out later when it's too late? Remember, marital difficulties may be like many diseases—readily treatable in early stages, but fatal when they have gone too far.

4. *I am afraid to check up on my relationship.*

Yes, many people are afraid to go to the doctor because he may verify problems that they suspect. Fear of examining a couple's relationship can result from an inability to disagree, an inability to communicate, or a fear of admitting the unresolved problems that are known to exist. Any or all of these shortcomings can destroy a relationship, yet you can learn ways to overcome them. Isn't it worth a try?

Most experts on adulthood and marriage agree that marital relationships go through cycles and phases. Such life stages are not unnatural and can best be handled by shifts or changes in the nature of your interaction with your partner. Self-examination of your marriage, therefore, is a way to recognize the natural evolution of life and to anticipate changes that are needed to prevent problems as well as to solve them.

Taking Stock of Your Marriage

The remainder of this chapter consists of exercises to help you do your own marriage check-up. Before you begin, here is some advice to help assure you that the process will work, and even be enjoyable.

1. Make sure that you and your partner *are both willing* to complete the exercises. Reread the introduction to

The Marital Check-Up

the chapter together. Set up an appointment when you both agree to work on the exercises. Choose a time when neither of you will feel pressured or preoccupied with other matters.

2. Schedule your check-up time for at least forty-five minutes, but feel free to work longer if it's needed and if you're comfortable with it.

3. Be flexible. If you begin the exercises and you are tired, or can't concentrate, or it just doesn't seem to be working out, reschedule your meeting for a later time. (If this happens every time you try to meet, however, it may be a sign that one or both of you is avoiding the process.)

4. Be relaxed. It is important, especially if you and your spouse are uneasy about embarking upon a close look at your marriage, to be relaxed when you begin. However, we recognize that a person cannot relax simply by being told to do so. So here is an exercise to help you relax.

First, flex your muscles to loosen up any sore spots. Some people tighten up across the shoulders and in the neck muscles that lead to the base of the skull.

Then, sit in a comfortable position in your favorite chair. Close your eyes and visualize the most beautiful scene you can remember—a beach, a lake, or snowclad mountains—preferably a place you and your partner have enjoyed together.

Breathe deeply, and as you exhale, let your muscles fall loose—your arms, your shoulders, your torso, your legs. Imagine yourself turning to jello, and concentrate upon the stillness within yourself.

After a few minutes of this, open your eyes. Most people, after such a period of relaxation, feel alert and revitalized. Now turn to the section in your workbook that corresponds to this chapter and make a page for each exercise. Then proceed to the first exercise in your marital check-up.

Self-Disclosure Questionnaire

This questionnaire contains a number of items about different aspects of self-disclosure. *There are no right or wrong answers.*

Read the statement, and in your workbook fill in the appropriate response from the 1 to 5 scale in the space provided to the right of each question. The thing to ask yourself for each of these questions is, "How free do I feel in disclosing myself to my partner?"

Do you feel free to disclose only those things about yourself that you feel good about? Or do you also feel free to disclose those things you're not so proud of? What is your level of openness with your partner?

How often do you disclose to your partner how you're feeling about the following areas of your life?

1	2	3	4	5
Never	Seldom	Sometimes	Often	Very Often

1. The aspects of my personality that I dislike.
2. My feelings, if any, that I have trouble expressing or controlling.
3. Things in my past or present that I feel ashamed and guilty about.
4. The kinds of things that make me angry.
5. What makes me feel depressed.
6. What makes me feel anxious and afraid.
7. What it takes to hurt my feelings.
8. The kinds of things that make me especially proud of myself, elated, full of self-esteem or self-respect.
9. How I wish I looked. My ideals for overall appearance.
10. Whether or not I have any health problems, for example, trouble with sleeping, digestion, female com-

plaints, heart condition, allergies, headaches, etc. Which ones are causing me problems now?

11. Whether or not I have any long-range worries or concerns about my health, for example, cancer, ulcers, heart trouble. Which ones are of concern to me?

12. My feelings about whether or not I feel able to relate well enough in sex relationships.

13. Problems I have had in relationships with my brothers and sisters.

14. Problems I have had in my relationship with my father.

15. Problems I have had in my relationship with my mother.

16. Feelings I now have toward my siblings.

17. Feelings I now have toward my father.

18. Feelings I now have toward my mother.

19. Concerns I have had about the relationship between my parents.

20. Concerns I have had about the role I played in the relationship between my parents.

21. Feelings I have had about the ways in which I seem to be like my father.

22. Feelings I have had about the ways in which I seem to be like my mother.

23. What I like most about my partner as a companion.

24. What I dislike most about my partner as a companion.

25. What I like best about my partner as a lover.

26. What I dislike most about my partner as a lover.

27. What I like most about the way my partner disciplines our child(ren).

28. What I dislike most about the way my partner disciplines our child(ren).

29. What I like most about the way my partner teaches our child(ren).

30. What I dislike most about the way my partner teaches our child(ren).
31. What I like best about the way my partner joins in family fun.
32. What I dislike most about the way my partner joins in family fun.
33. What I like best about the way my partner shares in family responsibility.

Now that you have completed this questionnaire, do you feel that you know yourself a little better? Were you surprised by the number of areas that you do not discuss openly with your partner? Each of these questions, of course, could become a topic of dialogue with your partner, but the function at this point was simply to reveal yourself to yourself.

Many people are amazed to discover how many intimate thoughts, desires, and angers they have locked away in little mental cabinets where they are kept away from their partner.

Madge, for example, had been married for eleven years when she came to me for counseling. After filling out the self-disclosure questionnaire, she came back to me to discuss it.

"It was uncanny," she said. "I felt like someone was groping around touching all my tender nerve ends. Some of the questions were right out front, where I spend a lot of time being angry but trying not to show it. Others were like deep bruises I never knew were there. The questions also stirred a great many emotions and gave me some twinges of anxiety. I wondered what would happen if I really opened up to my husband, and I also wondered what he might be writing about the same questions."

The Marital Check-Up
Analysis of Self-Disclosure Results

What if, in going over this questionnaire with your partner, you find there is very little that you are comfortable in sharing with your husband or wife, whether your feelings are positive or negative? Examine the reasons for this.

Is it that you don't trust him?

Has he ever used shared information against you?

Is it that you just do not relate on an intimate level?

Or is it that you've simply acquired the habit of *not* sharing personal information about yourself?

Answering these questions should provide you with some clues to how to share more of yourself with your partner—if this is something you'd like to do. You may need to build up greater mutual trust, and it may be a while before you come to believe that your partner will not take advantage of your vulnerable areas.

A good way to start is to reveal fairly safe intimate information, and then build up to revealing more sensitive information about yourself. In this way you will gradually build a higher level of trust. If your partner loves you, she will not want to hurt you by taking advantage of your vulnerabilities. You should find it satisfying, rewarding, exciting, and fun to relate on a more intimate level.

Before you actually begin, however, write down your thoughts about your hesitancy to reveal yourself—including your anxieties and fears—in your workbook.

Do You Really Like Yourself?

Following is another questionnaire, designed to reveal how well you like yourself.

Why is this important? Often we treat our partner, our co-workers, our relatives, our children poorly because we do not feel good about ourselves. It's as if we need an external target for our inner hostilities. We may speak harshly to our partner and he may wonder, "What did I do to deserve such wrath?" The truth is that he or she did nothing, perhaps, to merit your anger. Perhaps you were seething over something else—perhaps your own mistake or fault—but your partner served as a convenient target for the release of your feelings.

It is easier when you feel good about yourself to treat others in a civil manner. See how you rate on the questionnaire, then we'll discuss how to improve things. The first step is to identify problems. The next step is to try to find solutions. Answer the questions fairly and honestly.

Enter the number in your notebook which best describes how well you like yourself.

1	2	3	4	5
Never	Rarely	Seldom	Occasionally	Always

1. If someone hurts my feelings, I tell them so.
2. People value my opinions.
3. I feel intelligent.
4. Nothing is too good for me.
5. There's not much about me that I'd really like to change.
6. I find myself constantly comparing myself with other people to see if I rate higher than they or if they rate higher than I.
7. I enjoy meeting and talking with new people.
8. I feel like an outsider at a party.
9. There aren't many people I would change places with.
10. I find myself wishing I were someone else, somewhere else, doing something else.

The Marital Check-Up

11. If I had my life to live over, I wouldn't change much.
12. I like the place where I live.
13. I enjoy my work.
14. People generally admire me.
15. I'm a kind person.
16. I enjoy getting up in the morning.
17. I can take care of myself.
18. Other people need me.
19. I enjoy watching what I eat, getting proper exercise, and taking good care of myself.
20. I try to make sure I lead a balanced life—enough sleep, enough work, enough play.
21. I find time alone very frightening.
22. I enjoy my time alone.
23. I like myself.
24. I respect myself.
25. I value myself.
26. I see myself as an attractive person.
27. I see myself as a kind person.
28. I see myself as a loving person.
29. I see myself as a sharing person.

What if you find you don't feel good about yourself?

If this is the case, you have a lot of company. We live in a negative time and culture. It seems easier and more common for people to criticize themselves and others than it is to give positive strokes.

Look around you. How many people do you know who you would say have a totally positive self-concept? Probably very few. What can you do to start feeling better about yourself?

One thing is to become aware of the things you tell yourself. Do you get up in the morning, look in the mirror, and say, "God, what a mess!" Or do you look in the mirror, smile back at yourself, and say, "Good morning. This is going to be a glorious day."

You *really* have the power to make it a wonderful day or a miserable day and it can be done if you give yourself honest credit for the good things you do and the good things within you. It is hard to understand, but generally true, that we give ourselves no credit for the things we do well, but are sharply critical of the things we do wrong.

Most people do not realize the tremendous power they have to see positive rather than negative traits in themselves, and thus in life. Be kind to yourself. Be tolerant and nurturing. *You deserve it.* Treat yourself like a king or queen. You'll be amazed at how fantastic you can feel, what a natural high you can experience, if you start treating yourself like royalty.

It is axiomatic that you cannot love others well unless you first love yourself. This may sound self-indulgent but it really is not, because it leads to a better life—not only for yourself but for your partner and children as well.

I recall one man who held himself in very low esteem, and in any situation of conflict with his wife he tended to blame himself. Leonard tried to work against this tendency and finally discovered that he was judging himself according to the very harsh judgments his father had brought against him as a child.

"Dad used to whip me if I did something wrong," Leonard said, "and he called me a lousy brat. It didn't matter if it was a little thing or a big thing, he always jumped on me as if I had committed a major crime. I grew up feeling that I couldn't do anything right.

"So I guess I transferred that into our marriage. Finally, after taking the blame for everything for so long, I sat down one day and said, 'Hey, you can't be completely bad. You're not an evil person.'

"After that," Leonard continued, "I started playing a

game with myself. When something went wrong, I pretended to talk to another person. 'All right,' I said to myself, 'I didn't like what you did just then. I like *you* all right, but I don't like what you did.'

"This little exercise did wonders for me. Somehow it separated the deed from the person. After that I discovered that there was a pretty good guy there inside of me, and it made it a lot easier to correct the unpleasant things about myself."

Disagreement

Now that you've taken an honest assessment of yourself, the next thing to realize is that no close relationship can exist with another person without disagreement in some areas. If we are open in expressing our opinions and feelings, we are willing to agree and disagree *equally,* to express both our positive and negative feelings as equals.

Another questionnaire follows, this one to test your depth of feelings for agreeing or disagreeing with your partner. Again, there are no right or wrong answers for this questionnaire. It just gives you a better idea of how you see things and what you feel in your relationship with your partner. Once you have completed answering the twenty-two questions by yourself, compare answers with your partner. This can become a measure of the depth and completeness of your communication with each other as it becomes evident that you do not see your *interaction* in exactly the same way.

Dyadic Adjustment Scale

Answer each question as accurately as possible in your notebook.

5	4	3	2	1	0
Always Agree	Almost Always Agree	Occasionally Disagree	Frequently Disagree	Almost Always Disagree	Always Disagree

1. Handling family finances.
2. Matters of recreation.
3. Religious matters.
4. Demonstrations of affection.
5. Friends.
6. Sex relations.
7. Conventionality (correct or proper behavior).
8. Philosophy of life.
9. Ways of dealing with parents or in-laws.
10. Aims, goals, and things believed important.
11. Amount of time spent together.
12. Making major decisions.
13. Household tasks.
14. Leisure time interests and activities.
15. Career decisions.
16. How often do you discuss or have you considered divorce, separation, or terminating your relationship?
17. How often do you or your mate leave the house after a fight?
18. In general, how often do you think that things between you and your partner are going well?
19. Do you confide in your mate?
20. Do you ever regret that you married (or lived together)?
21. How often do you and your partner quarrel?
22. How often do you and your mate "get on each other's nerves"?

Continue now with the general appraisal of your marriage, each of you noting your answers in your workbook.

The Marital Check-Up

Marital Appraisal

The purpose of this exercise is to assess your current satisfaction in marriage.

A. Draw a line down the center of your paper. In the first column, list all the elements you like about your marriage, the things that *work well for you*. (Examples: *For the wife*—We have a beautiful home and furniture. My husband makes a good living. He is handsome and I enjoy being with him. *For the husband*—My wife is a good housekeeper. She is beautiful and we enjoy going out together. She is proud of my work.)

Now, in the second column of your page, list those elements which you dislike in your marriage and which *don't work for you*. (Examples: *For the wife*—We bicker about the children's behavior. He is stingy and doesn't allow me any freedom in spending money. *For the husband*—No matter how much money I give her, she squanders it. She's too easy with the kids.) Obviously, these examples are only the beginning of a list. Make it as extensive as you wish.

B. On a second page of your notebook, answer the following questions. It is important that each of you answers each one *in writing*.

1. Do you look forward to being with your partner after being separated during the day?
    a. If your answer is "no," write out the major reason why. Be specific. For example, "My partner immediately complains about what a mess the house is in, and asks me if I've wasted another day."
    b. If your answer is "yes," write down the reasons why your meeting at night is pleasant.

For examples, "The house is comfortable. The kids are glad to see me.

2. Define the word "love." Share your definition with your partner.

3. Does the word love mean that the security and well-being of your partner is as important to you as your own security and well-being?

4. Do you feel that your spouse loves you, no matter how you've defined love?

5. Briefly list what you feel are five instances of your own loving behavior toward your partner in the past month.

6. List what you feel are five instances of your partner's loving behavior toward you in the past month.

7. List five hateful things you have done—intentionally or unintentionally—to your partner in the past month.

8. List five hateful things your partner has done to you during the past month.

9. List five things you have asked your partner to correct or improve, but which he or she has not.

10. List five things your partner has asked you to change, but which you have not.

11. Of the items listed in your answer to question 10, which items could you have changed if you really wanted to? Which ones are you unwilling to change?

12. For each of the items listed in your answer to question 11, give your reasons why you are unwilling to make these changes.

13. For each item in question 9, list the reasons why you think your partner was unwilling to make these changes.

14. For the person who works, have you been getting along better or worse in your job since your marriage?

15. Describe in what ways you believe your marriage has been responsible for the answer you gave to question 14.

C. Discussion. Compare your answers from parts *A* and *B*. Conclude your discussion by answering *together* the following two questions.

1. Do we believe our marriage is less than we want it to be? (If the answer is "yes" from one or both, go on to question 2.)
2. Shall we find out what is wrong with the marriage, and try to improve it? (If the answer is "yes," go on to the next exercise.)

Interpersonal Comparison Tests

The purpose of this exercise is to assess individual feelings about self, marriage, and life.

A. Complete each statement below by selecting the answer that comes closest to your feelings *today*. Be sure that both of you answer *all* of the questions. Do the exercise separately, and *do not* compare notes until you both have finished.

Present Life Experiences

1. Financially and socially I feel the next five years
    a. will be reasonably successful.
    b. will consist of two steps forward and one back.
    c. are impossible to predict at present.
    d. scare me.
2. About my health, I would say that
    a. I have always had and expect to have perfect health.

  b. For the last few years, my general condition has been below par, but I believe I'll regain excellent health soon.
  c. I don't know for sure. I guess I'm as healthy as anybody, but I haven't had a physical for years.
3. About my psychological adjustment, I would say that
  a. I feel fairly secure emotionally.
  b. I am happiest not living alone.
  c. I probably do best living alone.
  d. I do not think about my emotions.
4. With regard to children,
  a. I have doubts about how good a parent I am.
  b. I know that I am a good parent.
  c. I would like to have at least four or five children.
  d. as far as I am concerned, my marriage would be most successful *without* any children.
5. With regard to being married at this particular time, I feel that
  a. since most of my friends are already married, I am glad I am too.
  b. marriage is an important stabilizing influence in my life.
  c. the person I wished to marry would not have waited if we had not married when we did.
  d. there was no special reason for marrying when I did, but I did not wish to disappoint my friends and relatives.
  e. it was as good a time as any to marry.

The Person I Am Married to

1. My partner's appearance
  a. is extremely attractive physically.

b. is not unusually attractive physically but is likeable.
   c. means little to me because he (she) is someone I do not think of in terms of physical attractiveness.
   d. embarrasses me.
2. My partner
   a. comes from a family I greatly admire.
   b. comes from a family I feel very much a part of.
   c. has so little family closeness that I feel sorry for him (her).
   d. has very irritating parents, but I can overlook them.
3. With regard to family similarities to the parents of my partner,
   a. I am worried that she may become too much like her mother (or he like his father).
   b. I am concerned that she may become too much like her father (or he like his mother).
   c. I do not feel his (her) parents play any significant role in our marriage.
   d. I do not think he (she) is like either of his (her) parents.
4. With regard to marriage, my partner and I
   a. have discussed our doubts and fears of marriage.
   b. have had some doubts, but have not mentioned them.
   c. may be afraid of hurting each other by bringing up the question of whether we have made a mistake.
   d. do not have any doubts whatsoever.
5. With regard to *our* marriage,
   a. I would like to leave it, but am afraid.
   b. despite my doubts I prefer to stay in it.

    c. I feel I can overcome any doubts since my love is great enough.
    d. I would have doubts no matter whom I had married, and therefore should not let these doubts stand in the way now.

Marriage and Profession

1. With regard to my occupational or avocational interests,
    a. I feel I have the courage to pursue both my marriage and my interests, even when they conflict.
    b. I feel I could sacrifice almost anything in order to have a happy marriage.
    c. I see no conflict between marriage and other interests.
    d. my partner has no ambitions or professional commitments which will jeopardize or interfere with our marriage.
    e. my partner's devotion to his (her) career is something I can admire and support.
    f. my partner's devotion to his (her) career is something I hope I can get more enthusiastic about as I understand him (her) better.
2. With regard to the future of our marriage,
    a. I am worried about becoming poor.
    b. I am worried about the influence of our in-laws upon us.
    c. I am troubled about how many children we should have.
    d. I sometimes think my partner might have an affair.
    e. I prefer not to worry about things until they happen.

3. With regard to companionship, my spouse and I
   a. have many interests in common.
   b. have independent interests, but are tolerant and supportive of each other's activities.
   c. expect to develop interests in common.
   d. seem to have little in common when we are not busy with social activities.

B. Discussion. After both of you have completed the questions, summarize the results by sharing your answers. How many did you answer the same? How many answers were different?

C. Discussion. Ask each other the following questions.

   1. How can we utilize our "sameness" to increase the solidarity of our marriage?
   2. How can we turn the differences into advantages or neutralize them?

Listening

The purpose of this exercise is to determine how *accurately* we listen to each other.

Limit each person to fifteen or twenty minutes for each step of the discussion. Do not attribute anything to your partner except what is actually said.

   1. One person begins talking by making statements that begin like this: "The characteristics I would like to see in you to make the marriage more workable are . . ."
   2. The second partner then summarizes the comments made by the first. Use "I" as the subject, such as, "It

seems to me that if I were in your position I would want me to be . . ." In summarizing what the first speaker has said, don't try to defend yourself or attack your partner. Simply restate what he or she has said.

3. Reverse roles. The partner who spoke first now listens as the other recites the characteristics he would like to see changed. Following this, the other partner summarizes the material, as above.

4. Repeat the same process, only this time the first speaker begins his talk by saying, "You contribute destructively to our marriage by . . . and you could improve the situation by . . ." The partner listens for up to fifteen minutes, then summarizes what he has heard. The roles are then reversed again.

Taking Directions

The purpose of this exercise is to learn to take direction from your partner.

Make sure that both partners complete the exercise at least once.

1. One partner will plan an entire weekend (two days and one night minimum). During this time, his partner will follow all suggestions and instructions.

2. One weekend later, the roles will be reversed. At the end of each day, express your feelings and thoughts.

3. How does it feel to be the leader? The follower? Is this different from the normal role you play? How did it feel to follow instructions without any opportunity to disagree or take charge?

The Marital Check-Up

Yes-No Inventory—Commitment

The purpose of this exercise is to measure the commitment each partner has made to remaining in the marriage and improving it.

Allow only "yes" or "no" answers, without qualification or embellishment. *Do not* discuss the answers at this time, but set a definite date, not less than five days from now, for a follow-up. (See the following exercise.) Both partners should answer the questions honestly.

1. Do you believe that this marriage can be improved?
2. Do you think our marriage is worth an investment of effort?

Yes-No Inventory—Discussion

Make sure you have done the previous exercise at least five days prior to this one. Do *not* use this as a format for argument.

Repeat the questions from the previous exercise.

A. Compare your answers with those you obtained five days earlier.

B. Each partner will ask a series of questions (listed below) aloud, and then answer each one as the other partner listens. Remember, this is not a discussion yet. One person asks a question of himself and answers it for himself. When the first partner has finished, the other partner does the same thing.

1. During the last few months, have I ever said, "If only you would _____, our marriage would be much better"?
2. In the last few months, have I often stated, "If

you had a different personality, I would be much better off and the marriage would be much smoother"?

3. Have I in the last few months used past history against you? Have I brought up your past errors and ways of behaving, things I didn't like about you in the past, in order to prove a point, or to intimidate you, or to get some degree of control over you? (Remember, these are all to be answered by the partner who is asking himself the questions.)

4. In the last few months have I generalized about some fault of the opposite sex? (Here the speaker should try to recall whether he has indulged in the common game of the battle of the sexes. It is easy to forget that our biases are reinforced constantly, and are thus enlarged, unless we become aware of the danger and guard against such games.)

5. In the last few months have I felt vulnerable in relation to you? (Only by avoiding a sense of vulnerability can one be open, fully trusting, and nondefensive. The speaker should try to remember if he has withheld loving behavior because it might be interpreted as approval of some disliked behavior by his partner.)

6. In the past few months have I used the children against you at any time?

Now, if you have each asked and answered these questions, it is time for a discussion in which you share your conclusions with each other.

Communication

The purpose of this exercise is to help you understand the status of communication in your relationship. Communi-

The Marital Check-Up

cation will be discussed in greater detail in a subsequent chapter.

Answer each question "yes" or "no," then explain what you mean and describe the situation in your marriage. This exercise may be done either by talking or by writing in your workbook.

1. Do you feel satisfied regarding your communication with your partner most of the time? Explain.
2. Is your partner a good listener?
3. Does your partner listen to both the content and the *feeling* of your communication?
4. Do you have difficulty communicating your feelings, thoughts, on any particular subjects?
5. Are you ever frustrated when you try to communicate? Why?
6. Do you ever feel good about your communications? When?

Time Priorities and Management

The purpose of this exercise is to assess your goals and priorities in life, and your use of time to achieve them. Time management will be discussed in greater detail in a subsequent chapter.

A. Answer the following questions in writing. Both partners should complete the answers without consulting each other.

1. What are your goals for the next year? Be specific. Think of work, family, school, money, personal appearance, etc.
2. What are the three things you most want to accomplish during the next year?

3. What are the obstacles to managing your time now?
4. What do you do best in terms of managing your time?
5. What are your biggest problems in managing time?
6. What does your partner do best in terms of managing time?
7. What are your partner's problems in managing time?
8. What goals for the next year do you think you share with your partner? For the next ten years?
9. How can your partner help you to achieve your goals?
10. How do you think you can help your partner to achieve his or her goals?

B. Discussion. Compare your answers with your partner's.

Sexual Relations Inventory

The purpose of this exercise is to assess your sexual relationship. This topic will be covered in greater detail in a subsequent chapter.

Write the answer to each of the following questions.

1. Is your sexual life satisfactory? ("Yes" or "no.")
2. Is there anything missing from your sex life? What?
3. What can you do to improve your sex life?
4. What can your partner do to improve your sex life?
5. Do you have any sexual problems? If you answer yes, please identify.

6. Does your partner have any sexual problems? If yes, identify.
7. Who do you think is responsible for your sexual pleasure? ("Both," "me," or "my partner.")
8. Do you have orgasms? ("Always," "sometimes," or "never.")
9. Who is responsible for your orgasm experience? ("Me," "my partner," "both," or "no one.")

The following questions are taken from Harlman F. Fihran, *Treatment of Sexual Dysfunction*.

10. What was the most memorable sexual event in your life?
    a. Who was responsible?
    b. What was your response?
11. What was the most disappointing sexual event in your life?
    a. Who was responsible?
    b. What was your response?
12. Who influenced your attitudes and sexual values?
    a. Church
    b. Home
    c. Peers
    d. Ethnic background
    e. Other
13. In terms of your appeal to sexual partners, do you see yourself as an attractive person?
    a. Are you more attractive now?
    b. Or as a child?
14. What are your greatest attributes?
    a. As a person.
    b. To your partner.
    c. To your children.
    d. In social situations.

15. Describe your sexual identity.
    a. Are you comfortable with your sexuality?
    b. Can your partner please you easily?
    c. Can you please your partner?
    d. Can you please yourself?

Conflict Summary

The purpose of this exercise is to identify specific problem areas in your marriage.

Create in your workbook a list of problem areas in your marriage. Begin by examining an entire week in your life. Look for certain times of the day or certain situations which have caused you anger or frustration. Which of your partner's behaviors are involved? Consider—but don't limit yourself to—the following categories, and list any conflicts that arise in these areas: sex, communications, children, money, vacations, leisure time, free time, meals, schedules, material possessions, friends, careers, and values.

Review all of the exercises you have done in this chapter and include any conflict areas that were revealed. Pay special attention to areas which either of you felt reluctant to discuss or which triggered arguments.

Your Own Special Problems

The marital check-up was placed early in this book because it is essential to identify the specific areas which need attention as you become your own counselor. In the ten exercises just completed you probably uncovered some areas that you would like to improve in your relationship.

Make sure that you and your partner *both* agree that a

The Marital Check-Up

certain action needs to be taken. It is important to find out if *both* of you are willing to work on the problem areas. If you have not done so before, affirm this point with your partner *now*. Meet with him or her. Share your ideas about what needs to be changed in your marriage. Listen as your partner tells you what he (she) believes needs to be changed. Determine if you both are willing to learn the skills necessary to make these changes. Find out what each of you has learned in conducting your marital check-up.

Now move on to the next chapter and begin to work on your relationship.

5
Creative Communication and Conflict Resolution

The most important element of any sound relationship is communication.

That flat statement may seem strange to you because most of us believe that we *are* communicating all the time—with our partner as well as with other people. The fact is that we habitually *tell* things to others and sometimes listen half-heartedly when they tell us something, but the actual communication is superficial and often meaningless. Part of the fault lies with the word communication, which does little to communicate its own meaning. It may help to examine its roots—the idea of *community,* of *communing* with another person. At that level, you see, communication becomes more than a discussion of the weather, the family finances, or world affairs. It implies a degree of depth and honesty.

The essential point we are trying to reach in a marriage is the ability to express to your partner what you *need,* what you *feel,* and how you *feel about him* or *her.* And it is equally important that we do this without damaging our partner's self-esteem.

We face the paradox that as infants we have the ability to communicate clearly what we want, such as crying when hungry or uncomfortable. Yet, when we outgrow the most basic mode of communication, we are often left without the tools and skills we need to communicate as adults. We learn to hide our needs and feelings rather than revealing them to our partner clearly and distinctly. At the same time, we unconsciously communicate nonverbally by tone of voice, facial expression, and body posture and gestures—so-called body language. The problem is that the message conveyed by body language sometimes does not match the content of verbal communication. The net result can be confusing to those receiving these "mixed messages."

As creatures blessed with the gift of speech, we still have the ability to clearly communicate what we need. We just have to learn to translate the cries and noises of infancy to verbal skills. If a baby can do it, you can do it, and clear, honest communication that doesn't conflict with other body language can help to cleanse many muddied areas of misunderstanding.

Steps in Effective Communication

Know Yourself

Don't hide your needs and feelings from yourself, be *aware* of them. Explore your fantasies and give them free rein within yourself, although some of them may be impossible to achieve. Hold silent dialogues with different aspects of yourself listening to what each facet of your personality feels. These can be tools to greater self-awareness.

For example, do you secretly yearn for a cabin in the hills with a simple, earthy lifestyle, rather than living in a crowded apartment with the noise and bustle of the city? Do you imagine yourself free of clothing on the beach or backpacking in the mountains, rather than reading books, watching television, or other passive indoor activities.

Do you like your body? Or have you been ashamed to *really* look at it and touch it. Remove your clothes and study yourself in the mirror. Look at your face and hair, your feet, your thighs and chest and muscles, the texture of your skin. Touch your skin and genital organs. Do you like what you see and feel, or would you rather be someone else? Are there things you could do to make yourself more handsome or beautiful? If so, honestly examine the reasons why you are not doing them.

We are not talking specifically about *changing* yourself at this point, but rather *knowing* yourself as you are and want to be. Even if circumstances make it impossible for you to fulfill your fantasies, it is important to be in touch with them.

One beautiful young woman found herself growing fat after two or three years of marriage. Sheryl was not aware of her real reasons for eating excessively, but she dreaded stepping on the scales each morning.

When she passed 150 pounds, she decided that something must be done, and her first step was to communicate with herself to learn why it was so difficult to change her diet. She did not like what she saw in the mirror and she knew that her husband did not like it either, although he had not made direct, critical comments. He *did* resent paying the bills when she was forced to change her wardrobe periodically.

In essence, Sheryl was not the physical person she had once been and wanted to be again. By thinking through her problem honestly, with no rationalizations or excuses, she came to realize that she was using rich, heavy food as compensation for a pleasure need. After a few months of marriage, her husband had gradually stopped paying compliments and verbally admiring her beauty as he had done before they were married. By eating to compensate for this loss (rather than telling him her need), Sheryl was not only indulging a need for gratification but also, subconsciously, punishing her husband for his lack of attention.

Actually, she did not come to grips with the idea of punishing him, but for her own satisfaction and to regain his admiration, she went on a diet.

Two weeks later, when she had lost fifteen pounds, her husband congratulated her for her effort, and let her know he admired her beauty. This reward more than compensated for her self-denial in food, but Sheryl's most important reward was an awareness of who she was, who she wanted to be, and who she could be. So by communicating with herself first, she was able to gain what she needed for and from herself *and* her husband.

Another good way to become more aware of yourself is to keep a journal. Earmark a section of your workbook as your diary. Each day—or as often as seems comfortable—write ideas, thoughts, needs, desires, fantasies in your workbook. That can be your stepping stone in getting to better know your feelings and your need to express them.

Sherod Miller and his coauthors in *Alive and Aware** give a simple way to answer the question "Who am I?" You are a different person at different times. You are the thinking you, the feeling, wanting, doing, and sensing you. Here's how Miller pictured it.

---

* The awareness wheel on the following page is taken from ALIVE AND AWARE: How to Improve Your Relationship Through Better Communication (1975, Dr. Sherod Miller, Elam W. Nunnally, Daniel B. Wackman; Interpersonal Communication Programs, Inc., 300 Clifton Ave., Minneapolis, Minn.).

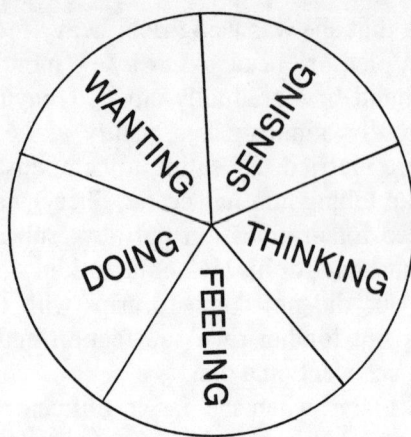

If you can increase your awareness of these five dimensions, you can know yourself better.

Each day, ask yourself exactly what you're experiencing at that particular moment. Sit down and summarize that impression in your workbook. Use the awareness wheel as a guide to see what areas you wish to reach at any given time. Try to get in touch with all aspects of yourself as pictured. Let all states of awareness flow freely. Don't try to write a masterpiece; you're probably the only person who will ever see this.

As you improve at this exercise (you should repeat it many times), try also to get in touch with your beliefs, conclusions, opinions, ideas, and expectations. They, too, are a part of you.

Watch Your Body Language

Often you communicate on a nonverbal level through your posture, body movement, voice intonations, facial expressions, gestures, and physical distance from the person with whom you're communicating. You may think you are communicating one thing when your partner is actually *receiving* something entirely different.

Check it out with him. One easy way to become aware of body language (and we are usually not aware of it) is to notice your facial expression when you tell someone you're angry with him. Next time you're angry, try to check your expression. If your face is pinched and tone of voice harsh, your body language matches your verbal communication. However, if you're smiling or even giggling when you say it, which mood should your partner pick up—your angry mood or your frivolous mood? Consider how confused you would be if the situation were reversed. In order to communicate precisely how you feel, you must align your expressions with your words.

More commonly, when one person is trying to hide an unpleasant feeling from another, the verbal and body language are at odds. An example is Harry, whose wife has been ill several times. Therefore, he is generally anxious about her health. She, in turn, is unhappy that she troubles him and, in fact, resents his often repeated queries about her health.

"When I ask her how she's feeling in the morning," Harry said, "she'll say 'Oh, fine,' but I know from the paleness of her face, the pinched expression, her clenched hands, that she isn't feeling well.

"Over the years I've learned not to press the point because I know she doesn't like me hovering over her like a mother hen. But then at other times, she is closed and cold and remote and I'm concerned that she is irritated by something I've done or failed to do. She will insist that this is not so, but her expression and manner tell me otherwise. Sometimes I won't find out until days later what was troubling her. In the meantime, I've gone through the agonies of trying to match what she says with the way she looks and acts. Am I supposed to be a mind reader?"

Once you've gotten in touch with how you feel, you

can see how important it is that your verbal and body language match when you communicate those feelings. You can see how important it is to express yourself clearly, honestly, directly, and that brings us to the next point.

Assert Yourself

Learning what you want to say is only part of the problem. Then you must learn to like and respect yourself and what you have to say. Make sure your partner understands clearly and directly what you *need*.

This does not imply arrogance or belligerence. It simply means that you should not hide your needs and desires out of concern for your partner's reaction. Often we hide our needs because we fear rejection.

Be Willing to Disclose Yourself

By opening yourself up, sharing yourself, and taking a chance in trusting your partner not to take advantage of your vulnerabilities, you pave the way for better communications and greater intimacy.

An example is Helen, whose husband is college educated and widely respected in the community. She had been forced to go to work after high school graduation and did not go to college. She felt intellectually inferior to her husband, and felt keenly embarrassed to join him at social gatherings where she knew there would be much intellectual discussion.

"One night we were going out," Helen said, "but I dreaded it. I can't honestly say that I had ever been put down by Dick's friends, but I always felt that sometime I would say something dumb that would embarrass him. That night I dawdled at the dressing table, somehow not able to get myself together to go out.

"Dick has always been exasperated when I'm late getting ready but tries not to show it. That night I was *really* late. He came in to the bedroom and said, 'Hey, aren't we going to make it tonight?' I burst into tears.

"Dick took me in his arms and gentled me, thinking something awful was wrong and then, before I had a chance to get my shield up again, I was blubbering out all my feelings of intellectual inferiority and embarrassment. Dick was amazed. He had no idea I had been laboring under this burden of concern and uneasiness all these years.

"First off, he called our host for the evening and said we couldn't come. Then we both got into comfortable clothes and spent the evening with a jug of wine talking out the whole thing. God, it was a relief for me, like taking a laxative and cleaning out an old accumulation of crud.

"As we talked, Dick assured me that never once had he been embarrassed of me in public and, in fact, he thought I always held up my end of any conversation very well. Besides, he said—and I know he meant it sincerely—a college education does not guarantee a person will be clever and wise. On the contrary, he thought I had done a better job of continued learning about the important things of life than most of the glossy bitches who talked so glibly about the esoteric books they'd read or the state of political affairs in Timbuktu.

"I needed that. Lord, how I needed it. I never loved Dick more than I did that night and we would never have had that lovely intimacy if I hadn't been literally forced to open up and tell him my problem. And now that I know how *he* feels about it, I face his intellectual friends with head up and with much more confidence than I ever had before in my life."

The Skills of Empathetic Listening

One part of effective communication is opening up and revealing your needs, fears, and desires to your partner. The other half is to really *listen and hear* what he has to say. It may be just as difficult for him to open up as it is for you, so you need to concentrate on both his verbal and body language to understand what is happening. And beyond understanding is empathy, that state of comprehension where you can say, "Darling, I understand what you're saying and I can almost feel the way you are feeling. I promise not to hurt you with these private things you've told me." Learn to listen for feedback from your partner when you have told him something very important to you. That will indicate to you whether or not he hears and feels how much this means to you.

Nonjudgmental Communication

Think about how much of the communication between you and you wife or husband is judgmental. How often do we hear, "Can't you ever keep this house cleaned up?" or "Why do you always come home late when you know I have dinner ready at six?" When we make a "you" statement, more often than not we are blaming our partner or judging him for something he has done.

You can avoid this and improve your relationship by using "I" statements instead. This way you can tell your partner how his actions affect you without loading him with a burden of guilt. For example:

1. *Blaming.* Don't say, "You made me angry and impatient with you . . ." Rather say, "I feel angry and impatient when you . . ." In this way, you take responsibility for your anger, and do not shift that responsibility onto the other person.

2. *Interrogation.* "Where were you last night? It was past midnight when you got home, wasn't it?" That is an accusatory interrogation. Such an approach immediately puts the other person on the defensive.

A better way to deal with this situation is, "I was really worried last night when you didn't get home by nine as you said you would. I realize it's tax season and hard for you to know when you can break away, but I would appreciate a call if you see you're going to be late."

Here you have made a simple request, and one that's easy for your partner to satisfy.

3. *General, vague pronouns.* Sometimes we communicate by using "it" or "we" or "they." This is overgeneralizing. You are really expressing your own feelings by attributing them to some other individual(s). This may be presumptuous. The other person may not really have the feelings you ascribe to him but doesn't want to contradict you. Therefore, he or she doesn't get the chance to communicate his or her feelings. The tendency, then, is for that person to avoid talking about what he or she feels.

It's best for each person to speak for himself. This can be accomplished by using "I" messages. Try it, and practice it.

Exercises in Communication

Following is a series of exercises designed to help raise your level of awareness in communication.

Communications in Silence

It is impossible for you *not* to communicate. Even silence is a way of communicating.

- Silence can be a time of intimacy, closeness, feeling through touch.
- Silence can be a time of anger and tension.
- Silence can express withdrawal from each other.
- Silence can be an expression of distance, dislike, separateness.
- Silence can be used as punishment. The partner who breaks verbal contact may feel, "I did not get what I wanted, so I will punish him (her) by not talking."

The following exercise will help you to become more aware of the power of silence. Sit facing each other, without speaking, and look into each other's eyes. Start with thirty seconds, then one minute, and finally two minutes. Afterward, share your thoughts and feelings during the silent period with your partner.

In the future, when you are both silent, be aware that *you are communicating a message of some kind*. Translate the silence into words and consider your silence as valuable communication time. Try to understand what happens to you and how your partner feels about your silence. Learn to listen to the silences as well as the words.

Communication through Your Body

Your body communicates continuously. It has its own powerful language. Whether you use words or not, your body communicates independently. Words transmit your message on one level, while your body involuntarily reveals your thoughts, feelings, and attitudes on another level. These are shown by the way you move, sit, stand, and by your gestures and facial expressions. Be aware of this. Learn to observe, respond to, and listen to your own body, so you'll know what it is saying to your mate, and what his (her) body is communicating as well.

Creative Communication and Conflict Resolution

As a test, before you and your partner go to your next cocktail party, agree to check out with each other your own and his (her) *real* mood during certain times of the evening. For example, if your partner seems to be listening to a joke that his boss is telling, but has a forced smile and is facing partly away from his boss as if trying to find an escape, check with him shortly afterward. Was he really interested in what Roger was saying, or was the boss telling a joke he's told thirty-two times before? You'll learn to be sensitive to his body cues.

Closeness vs. Distance

Sit near your partner while you talk to him or her about something personal. Then move away about three feet and try to find a comfortable distance for both of you. Move closer again—six inches apart—and make eye contact. How does it feel now?

Your body has a "safety" zone; if another person invades your private territory, you feel tense and restless. You need to move away. Each person's zone is different. There isn't any right or wrong amount of space you might need.

Now turn your backs to each other, face in opposite directions, and tell each other something personal. How does it feel to talk about an intimate subject without eye contact?

Finally, hold hands while you talk and look into each other's eyes. Touch each other another way, and then say the same thing without touching and without eye contact. Do you notice the difference? Share it with your partner. You're learning how much space each partner needs to communicate effectively.

In the communication process, you relate on two levels. One level is *content,* the meaning of the words that are said. The second level is *process,* the feelings that are conveyed with the words. The feelings can be conveyed by tone of voice, facial gestures, posture, or timing.

For example, a wife tells her husband she's depressed because of an unpleasant incident at work. He comments, "That's too bad," but continues to read his newspaper. The process is reading the paper, indicating disinterest in her problem, while answering perfunctorily. The two levels of communication—content and process—are *incongruent.* They do not match; they are inconsistent. For clear communication, the process and content need to match, to be congruent and consistent.

Speak for Yourself

This is an opportunity to practice what we discussed earlier regarding "I" statements. Begin all of your remarks with "I" rather than with "we" or "you." Your togetherness will be demonstrated by sharing, helping, and doing things for and with each other. When you wish to express your opinions or feelings, don't talk for your partner. Don't say, "We always like to be together." "We" is an assumption. Perhaps you do, but he or she does not.

Negotiation

Here we begin discussion of one of the most essential aspects of a good, working marriage—the art of negotiation. We trust that by now you have absorbed the previous exercises and practiced them, because there can be no successful negotiation without good communication. And by negotiation we refer to the ability to find a mutual solution to a problem without either party feeling that he or she has *won* or *lost*. There are six basic stages to negotiating resolutions.

1. Define the area of disagreement.
2. Stay in the present (don't dredge up the past) and negotiate *one problem at a time.*
3. Take turns expressing how you feel about the problem and your suggested solutions. Use "I" messages.
4. Compromise with a *new* solution, taking into account what both of you want.
5. Discuss in detail how the solution will be carried out.
6. Decide that after a certain trial period you will reevaluate the solution to see if it is doing the job or if you need to renegotiate a new solution.

Let's take a closer look at the reasons for these six steps in negotiating compromises.

You need to *define the area of disagreement* because often, in the stress of anger, people explode and bring in other past unresolved problems. Insist upon discussing only the problem that exists now. Agree to discuss those other problems at another time, if you wish, but right now talk about only the problem at hand. It is important to *stay in the present* and not counterattack with another problem. Focus on one at a time.

In each negotiating process there is an element of compromise—finding a new solution acceptable to both parties, a solution in which no one wins or loses. Both of you emerge as winners. The solution does not result from one person manipulating the other or one using power over the other.

The zero to ten scale is a useful device to apply in measuring how important the issue may be to each partner.

If to one person the problem and the solution he is suggesting are mildly important, he might rate it a 2; whereas, if the other partner feels strongly about the problem and *his* suggested solution, you might rate his need as a 9. The suggestion of the partner with the stronger feelings should be given greater weight in balancing this particular compromise. However, this presumes that both husband and wife are totally honest in expressing the depth of feeling. Otherwise, either one or the other could use this scale as a manipulative tool to control the compromise.

After you have reached a new decision together, the way you follow through with it is vital. If you fall short at the implementation stage, you are right back at the beginning. You have only worked it through halfway. Later evaluation of the compromise and how it is functioning is also important. If your solution is not working, you both need to be aware of it. Otherwise, again, you have not really solved the original problem. The important thing is that when you successfully negotiate and implement a workable solution to a problem, you both come out winners.

What Kind of Negotiator Are You?

There are various styles of negotiating. Observe and rate yourself and your partner by copying the exercise in your workbook and circling the numbers that you feel are appropriate. Compare your ratings with each other. Do you see yourself as your partner sees you?

1 = Not at all
2 = A little
3 = Moderately
4 = Very

Creative Communication and Conflict Resolution

Negotiation style	I am	He (she) is
Manipulative		
Leading		
Following		
Passive		
Threatening		
Peacemaking		
Rational		
Persuasive (influential)		

Questions to ask yourself:
1. Who makes most of the decisions?
2. Do you feel free to assert yourself and to say "no"?
3. Are you threatened by your partner's behavior?
4. In what way would you like your partner to change his negotiation style?

Role Reversal

In order to facilitate complete and honest communication, try to see a problem from the other person's point of view. Complain about something that bothers you and let your partner respond spontaneously. Now exchange roles. Let him repeat your complaint and you can hear it from his point of view. Keep in mind that there are many positions to *see, understand,* and *resolve* with any problem.

Good communications may seem simple to accomplish, but when you take all the variables into consideration, it really is not all that simple. You may believe that you are already communicating effectively when, in fact, you are not. How can you know?

One way to find out is to check with the person you're trying to reach. Another indicator of effectiveness is whether or not you are getting what you want and need. The problem may be that you do not ask for what you want. Or, you might ask, but in such an unclear way, that the other person cannot give you what you want, even if he wishes to do so. He must wade through layers of hidden meanings before he can perceive what you really want.

Here are some "skill" questions to ask yourself, and each other, to see how well you're communicating.

1. Do you form your thoughts clearly?
2. Are you really saying what you want to say?
3. Are you using superfluous words to get your meaning across?
4. Are you using too few words—leaving gaps, making assumptions—in stating your position?
5. Do you skip around haphazardly, or stick to one subject before going on to the next?
6. Are you willing to clarify your meaning if your partner says he doesn't understand?
7. Are you being congruent (consistent in words and body language) in what you're trying to communicate?

You can evaluate your listening skills, too, with the following questions.

1. Are you really listening to and hearing what your partner says, or are your thoughts wandering?
2. Do you question your partner when she says something you don't understand?
3. Can you allow for differing opinions or do you try to persuade your partner to "see it my way."
4. Do you listen *completely* to what your partner says, or are you busy thinking of your response while she's still presenting her views?

5. Can you allow your partner to finish his train of thought, or do you repeatedly interrupt?

If either of you answers part or all of these questions negatively, practice again the communication skills in this chapter and keep taking the test until you can honestly answer "yes" in every case. Send messages and listen actively. If you find your thoughts tend to scatter while your partner is presenting his view, try repeating his statement to see if you understand him correctly.

For example, if he says, "I feel that our sex life is lousy and we should do something about it," then she could ask, "Do I understand you to say that you don't enjoy our sexual relations and that we should do something to improve them?" If he agrees, you may continue with the discussion; if not, he needs to restate his position and you need to *listen*.

The Value of Conflict

Even with good communication skills between partners, conflict will arise now and then. In fact, as we have said, intimacy leads inevitably to conflict situations. You cannot maintain a level of intimacy without occasional disagreement. If you believe you have an intimate relationship, but say, "John and I never argue; we never fight," then chances are that your relationship is *not* intimate.

One reason that you may believe it is right to always "keep the peace" and never engage in upsetting confrontations is that society seems to place such a high value on this condition. It is only in the last decade or so that some people have begun to question that value—peace at any price. Dr. George Bach, author of *The Intimate Enemy: Creative Aggression,* has conducted considerable research in the area of "constructive aggression." He states that "couples who fight together are couples who stay together—provided they know how to fight properly."

He describes fighting unfairly or dirty as gunny-sacking. In gunny-sacking, the two partners accumulate and hide their grievances. Then a trivial incident will be sufficient for one or both to haul all of the old hurts and angers into the argument. Typically, in this kind of unfair fight, partners will try to hurt each other by attacking vulnerable points. If they have been close, each knows all too well how to "push the other partner's buttons." A woman who wants to hurt her insecure husband may attack his masculinity. He might retaliate by calling her a bitch. She might escalate by accusing him of being a poor provider and he might counterattack by accusing her of poor housekeeping, and so on, *ad infinitum*. Obviously, only a few seconds of this kind of fighting will obscure the original subject completely.

To prevent gunny-sacking, keep all arguments fair and up-to-date. Set aside some prime time each day to air your grievances on a regular basis. Couples who fight *regularly* and *constructively* don't need to carry gunny sacks full of complaints and bring the past into every argument.

Fight Inventory

Fights fall into a consistent and repetitive pattern because most couples fight about the same things most of the time. They may use different words, but their behavior and reactions are predictable. Now, using your workbook, remember and summarize your big and little fights of the past. What is the common denominator among them?

Are you fighting over trivial matters? Many couples do. For example, the man might repeatedly complain about cobwebs, dust, and dirt smudges in the house. His wife may be irritated by his failure to shave or hang up his clothes on weekends. Obviously, these are not major conflicts. A minor irritation is a "drop in the bucket," but if there are many accumulated drops in the backet, the couple's fight threshold grows low. Think about things that irritate you and tell your partner, no matter how trivial. Write them in a list in your workbook and compare notes. Level with each other and do not let trivial annoyances accumulate.

The Value of a Productive Fight

In a productive argument, several things are accomplished:
- Feelings are aired.
- Each person lets the other know where he stands.
- Each gains new knowledge about the other or a situation that involves them both.
- A level of renewed or deeper intimacy is reached.
- A workable compromise or solution is found.

If, after a fight, one partner feels like the winner and the other feels like the loser, what have we gained? The answer is, nothing but a pompous winner and a resentful loser. However, if both partners feel like winners, feel they have gained something, then it was a fair, productive fight. For this to work, both must win. This means you each must practice negotiating skills—even for the smallest disagreements—such as whether to eat out tonight or stay home. If you negotiate on small disagreements, you'll get into the habit for the main ones.

Fighting as Catharsis

Couples may fight simply to release tension. In this type of fight, the two are not requesting change from each other and there is nothing to win or lose. The topic and form of this fight may be the same time and time again. This ritualistic encounter, Bach labels a "round robin." It goes nowhere and the antagonists wind up at an impasse. If release of tension is what they're seeking, and an impasse is where they want to be, that is fine. However, if they wish to move beyond impasse, Bach suggests three steps:

1. Agree to a moratorium on all repetitive fighting.
2. Introduce a specific change so that the cause of the fight cannot happen again. (For example, a wife may complain that they sleep all day Sunday because they go to bed too late on Saturday night. They could agree to go to bed earlier and get up earlier on Sunday.)
3. Determine the real reason for the round robin fight. (In the above example, the wife really wanted to make love on Sunday morning instead of sleeping. Her real complaint was that her husband was not giving her enough physical satisfaction.)

Keeping Distance

At times, one function of a fair fight is that of regulating the emotional distance between two partners. Perhaps they have been close together a great deal and one (or both) feels his "style" is being cramped. He doesn't have enough space to "do his own thing." He may set up a fight (subconsciously) in which the outcome will be that each will retreat from the other for a while, giving both more space. A close relationship challenges that delicate balance between intimacy and suffocation. Each partner needs comfortable closeness and distance. You need to leave each other space to grow, but not enough space to destroy the intimate quality of your relationship. As Gerald Smith and Alice Phillips point out in *Me, You and Us,* "If a 'coming together' is the essence of true closeness, it follows that this cannot be achieved without occasional distance."

Couples who have too much togetherness and intimacy are advised to take a *vacation from marriage.* I suggest this when I see couples who seek distance from each other but are hesitant to express it. Each can go away alone for a few days, or go on vacation with another couple, or at the very least spend a day or an evening apart. Often, both partners will feel refreshed, renewed, and more intimate when they are reunited.

To recapitulate some of the principles expressed earlier, here are the elements of a fair fight:

1. *Observe your partner's vulnerabilities and respect them.* Do not try to attack or destroy.
2. *Stick to the real issues.* (Am I really angry at my husband for spending too much money on the kids, or because he refused to let me buy new carpeting for the living room?)
3. *Choose a good time for the fight.* Do *not* pounce when your partner is physically or emotionally worn out.
4. *Level with your partner.* Be honest about your feelings for him and for the issue of disagreement.
5. *Get feedback from your partner.* Listen actively, send "I" messages, confirm what you have heard, and work together toward a solution.

The fair fight is an open confrontation in which both partners are straight, open, and equal. Both listen openly, not defensively. Each genuinely wants to know what the other needs and requests.

Avoiding Confrontation

Why do we avoid confrontation? It seems so simple to tell our partner, straightforwardly and honestly, that we like or dislike something, or need something. Yet we often avoid such confrontations which could solve many problems before they grow severe. Often we avoid confrontation because we have learned that aggression, conflict, and anger are dirty words and taboo. Nice, intelligent people, we are told, do not raise their voices in anger. Yet we cannot stress often enough that partners who do not fight do not have an intimate relationship. In the dead marriage, no one fights or disagrees because neither *cares enough* for the other. In an honest, vital relationship, fighting serves a definite function and has its place.

Do you avoid your partner when he or she is angry?

Obviously, no one wants to be near an angry partner who yells and screams. You have the right *not* to respond to a shouting person, because anyone can make a decision to express his anger assertively rather than aggressively.

However, if you regularly avoid settling an argument just because you are uneasy about bringing up the subject, you are not being fair to yourself or your partner. Think about whether or not you are avoiding confrontation. Be honest with yourself.

Because confrontation is so scary, we often go out of our way to avoid it. Here are some of the ways we do so:

1. Hide behind a newspaper or television.
2. Ignore what your partner is saying. Remain silent.
3. Fall asleep. ("I'm too tired to discuss it.")
4. Develop a psychosomatic headache or stomach ache.
5. Change the subject.
6. Delay the matter. ("Let's talk about it later.")

Unfortunately, later never comes.

7. Give something else a higher priority. ("The children need me," or, "The yard needs to be mowed.")
8. Communicate a body message of "leave me alone."
9. Say "yes" just to end the discussion. This is accommodation.
10. Discuss trivial things to avoid the real issue. This is emotional divorce.

None of these is a permanent solution for avoiding conflict. They may be effective temporarily, but then you reach a point where you must deal with your differences. If you don't, you'll find yourself in an emotional vacuum.

As an exercise, for two weeks write in your workbook *each day* the methods you used to avoid potentially unpleasant situations with your partner, children, or friends. Observe your partner and keep a log on *his* confrontation avoidance techniques. At the end of the two weeks, discuss each of your workbook entries, and consider ways to be more direct with each other.

The alternative, if you remain together, is emotional divorce.

Emotional Divorce

Total conflict avoidance leads to that strange never-never land which can be described as a dead marriage because it never involves genuine intimacy. Partners relate to each other in a light, superficial, inconsequential manner. They do not level with each other, and they do not fight. A typical dialogue between such partners might go like this:

SHE: How was your day, darling?
HE: Fine, thank you. How was yours?
SHE: Okay. Do you want a drink before dinner?
HE: Good idea. I'd like the usual on the rocks.

SHE: Strong or weak?
HE: Whatever you mix. It doesn't matter.
SHE: What do you want to do tonight?
HE: Whatever you wish. It doesn't matter to me.
SHE: I'll join you. You know I don't care, as long as you're happy.

In this nice, peaceful home, nothing more meaningful is said all evening. The two might continue their routine with:

Shall we watch TV?
Do you want the newspaper?
It's time to go to bed. Good night, dear.

And then they are ready to start another lovely, peaceful—and empty—day, and another, and so on, forever.

These people have cut themselves off from creative communication. They have trained themselves never to discuss a subject which might involve disagreement, and thus involve something meaningful to either or both of them. Emotionally, they have moved away from each other. Emotionally, they now live in separate houses.

Related to emotional divorce, in which both partners avoid conflict, is *accommodation*. This means that husband or wife agrees to go along with any situation in order to avoid friction. In some ways, this may be worse than emotional divorce because it means that one of the partners seldom, if ever, gets what *he* wants. Such one-sidedness almost inevitably leads to dissolution of a marriage. Following is an example of accommodation:

SHE: My sister and her children will be coming to visit this summer, perhaps stay a month. Won't that be fantastic?

HE: (Looks angry but says) Yes, dear. That will be great. (He thinks, I hate those brats. There's never a minute's peace while they're here, but I'll do anything for the sake of peace because I can't stand hassling with her.)

SHE: (Visibly triumphant, thinks, I got what I wanted again. All I have to do is be charming and tell him at the right time, and I win.)

HE: (Resenting his wife and churning inside, thinks, my God, if she really loved me, she'd know how I hate having her sister and the kids stay with us.)

But he says nothing more, the company will come and he will be miserable because he could not force himself to resist his wife's wishes. His resentment will build and ultimately he'll have to leave the relationship or learn to "own up" to his angry feelings.

As another feature of this small marital interchange, the husband thought his wife should have been able to guess what he was feeling. Don't assume that your partner can guess what you want. *Never* assume or guess. *Always* inquire and check out your impressions.

The "Nice" Guy

The always agreeable person—and there are many of them—has been trained to shun anger as a bad thing and encouraged to be "nice" all the time. Not only is this a constant strain on him, it is an unrealistic goal. The nice guy is the accommodator just described. What does he fear? He is afraid of:
- expressing anger,
- being assertive,
- being rejected,
- confronting directly,

- dealing with conflict,
- not being loved.

He believes total agreeability is the only way to avoid conflict, or at least the best way for him. Perhaps he's afraid his feelings are ugly so he hides them. He is, in fact, doing himself a disservice. He hurts himself in these ways:

1. He is alienating himself from his partner. By not sharing how he really feels, he maintains distance between them.

2. He resents having to be nice and not being able to be frank and honest. He resents himself, the situation, and his partner.

3. He will probably repress his frustration until he can no longer maintain the facade. He will then explode, probably over a trivial matter. Or else he may simply leave his home and partner.

Perhaps needless to say, if either partner in a couple is a nice guy, the marriage will be virtually meaningless until he changes his ways and expresses himself assertively and straightforwardly. If *your* partner is a nice guy, realize that most of your victories are hollow and help him to level with you. This will make for greater intimacy in your relationship.

The Silent Treatment

The final form of conflict avoidance that we will discuss is passive-aggressive behavior—the silent treatment. This happens frequently between partners who are angry with each other, but are afraid to express it. They pretend everything is all right and avoid honest confrontation through silence. For example:

SHE: Dear, I waited two hours to have dinner with you. Finally, I ate alone. I didn't know when you were coming home. (Thinks, I'm angry with you, you bastard. You never come home on time. I don't know where you spend your time after work. You don't care at all about me. I wish you did.)

HE: That's okay darling, as long as you ate a good meal and were not hungry. (Thinks, I work hard all day and what does she do? Why can't she at least wait and serve me a warm dinner, the bitch! She's really got it easy around here. He is so angry he picks up the paper and ignores her.)

SHE: (Feeling left out, asks timidly) Darling, I want to tell you about my mother. She called today. (She waits for response from her husband. All she gets is silence. She tries again.) Darling, mother is sick and needs my help. She asked me to come tomorrow. I told her I would ask you first. Is it all right with you if I go? (More silence. Now she's convinced he is angry with her. She musters up the courage to ask what is bothering him.) Dear, are you angry with me?

HE: No. Everything's fine.

SHE: I thought maybe you were.

HE: I am tired, though. (He closes his eyes.)

SHE: I'm happy you can relax and rest. (Thinks, Here we go again, back to the silent treatment. She covers him with a blanket.)

The result of this entire interchange was that no one expressed his or her real feelings. Nothing at all was accomplished in terms of their relationship except that a greater reservoir of resentment was stored up in both.

It should be clear by now what we mean by good communication. It remains for you and your partner to practice it. The skills you develop will be crucial to your progress through the chapters to come.

6
Sex: Myth and Reality

Just as we need to sort out the myths of marriage in order to get to the realities, so the myths of sex continue to thwart genuine love-making, even in this age of so-called enlightenment and liberation.

It is puzzling that this should be true. We are inundated with thousands of books, magazine articles, and television shows devoted to sex—both new attitudes toward it and also techniques of love-making. Often it seems people are bewildered rather than enlightened by all the information they're receiving. Sex is one of the most difficult subjects for a man and woman to communicate clearly. One reason, of course, is that people are unique—each brings his or her own desires to love and must learn to apply theory to his or her ways of giving and receiving pleasure.

With the advent of women's liberation and the re-evaluation of male/female roles, American culture has been in a state of flux for the past ten years. It's an exciting time to be alive, but confusing as well, especially to those who have lived a major part of their lives under traditional rules and roles of sexual behavior, but are now being exposed to new ways. For instance, it is easier to accept the idea of trial marriage and casual sexual encounters at thirty than at fifty. The older woman has more built-in prejudices and mores to contend with than her younger counterpart. Likewise, it's probably easier for the person of thirty to experiment with unusual love expressions than it is for one of fifty.

The changes in what goes on between partners are principally changes in attitude; attitudes have broadened. It seems now that anything goes and anything can be discussed. Theoretically, at least, sex is no longer a taboo subject, except for those who resist change. In fact, the pendulum has swung from the extreme of puritanical inhibition and repression to the opposite of preoccupation with sex.

In spite of all this change in *attitudes,* we have *not* seen a change in the sexual *expression* between partners. People are "doing" the same things they've been experiencing for thousands of years, with one major difference—with open awareness of sex pervading our culture—from advertising to pornography—men and women are even more disturbed when their own private sexual experience fails to live up to the new models.

There are basically three ways to have sexual intercourse:

1. He does it *to* her (or she *to* him).
2. He does it *for* her (or she *for* him).
3. They enjoy it *with* each other.

It seems obvious that the more we depart from the sex object attitude implied in the first, and move toward the equality of the third, the better physical love will be. Yet all of this gets muddled and confused because we're stuck with the old myths about sex.

What are these myths?

Myth #1: Men "need" sex.

Because men are usually more quickly aroused than women (especially *young* men), this myth supposes that a man will suffer physical pain if he doesn't relieve his sexual tension. Certainly, in many young men, semen production does build a certain pressure, but this is naturally relieved in nocturnal emissions (wet dreams) or by masturbation.

The notion that "men need sex" (implying that women do not) can debase the beauty of love-making to the level of elimination as a body function.

Myth #2: Sex is a woman's duty to her husband

As the corollary to myth #1, the "duty" of sexual intercourse reduces the woman to the function of receptacle for a man's evacuation of semen, regardless of whether or not this is pleasant for her.

Myth #3: The man should always initiate sexual intercourse.

This myth is so old that it almost seems "natural," that is, that it is instinctive for man always to be the aggressor. The other half of this myth is that the woman should always be the passive receiver, that she should never suggest, by words or body language, when and how she would like to make love. Many marriages have been splintered by the fact that one partner or the other believed the two roles should never change.

Myth #4: The woman should keep her man guessing, in suspense.

This is the coyness game. The woman is supposed to be a mysterious creature, whose moods cannot be fathomed by the insensitive male. This game is no more than a roadblock to complete and open communication. One complaint I hear often from husbands is, "I never know if she wants me or not. She never gives a sign. I may start to make love to her and then find that she really doesn't want it. Then I feel like a fool.

"Or else she wants sex, but for some reason I don't detect her signals. Am I supposed to be a mind reader, for God's sake?"

Myth #5: He is responsible for her pleasure. He does it to her.

This links to the aggressor/passive receiver myth. This involves the woman (and they are legion) who challenges her husband to *give* her pleasure, sometimes, perversely, even against her will. She is saying, in effect, "It's *your* duty to make me feel *good.*" She takes no responsibility for her own pleasure.

Myth #6: He is always—and instantly—ready for sex.

This myth grows from the fact that during youth—from about ages fifteen to twenty-five—many men *are* ready for sex at any hour of the day or night. In a prolonged relationship, however, there are many times and many reasons when and why a man doesn't want to make love, or cannot.

We seem to accept the fact that a woman has a range of positive and negative moods, but expect the man to always come on as the ever-ready, aggressive male. The difference is pointed out more sharply by the fact that a woman's external signs of readiness for love are less evident than a man's. If he doesn't exhibit an instant erection, his mate often assumes that "he doesn't love me anymore."

The necessity for male erection, of course, is another myth. Many couples have learned that tender and beautiful physical love can be achieved in many ways, even if the man does not have an erection at all.

Myth #7: She has the power of veto. She is the judge of whether or not he is a good lover.

This is the surest and quickest way to castrate a man. In an intimate relationship, judging or evaluating is a negative attitude that damages intimacy.

Myth #8: He is responsible for her orgasm during intercourse.

Two words involved in understanding this myth are "responsive" and "responsible." A man and woman should be responsive to each other's needs, but each is *responsible* for his or her own orgasm.

Myth #9: There is only one way for a woman to reach orgasm.

For women, there are various ways to reach an orgasm that can be just as relaxing and satisfying *with or without* intercourse.

Much research in recent years indicates that perhaps a majority of women do not achieve orgasm through simple coitus. In no sense does this mean that the male is an inadequate lover. Rather, it indicates that they should use their ingenuity, using hands, mouth, or other objects to stimulate her to orgasm. He may do this, or she may do it for herself.

Myth #10: "The Big O"—the perfect orgasm—should occur simultaneously.

This myth was preached as gospel some years ago by many sex therapists and advisers. The idea was that perfect sexual expression occurred only when a man and woman reached orgasm at the same moment *during* intercourse.

This rarely happens, and it is not necessarily ideal. In concentrating so hard upon trying to time your orgasm to your partner's, you may not appreciate much of the pleasure in getting there. It is better to concentrate upon your own orgasm, one at a time, and let this intense feeling flow freely.

Myth #11: She is the judge of how long he should last.

We hear much about premature ejaculation, a common male sexual dysfunction, but we seldom examine whether or not it is a genuine dysfunction. How long should a man be able to last before he comes in intercourse? Ten seconds? Five minutes? Thirty minutes? Two hours?

No two people are the same and every couple should strive for mutual loving, not judgment of how long or how much the partner has to offer. If she is always the judge of how long he should perform, she may kill the sexual relationship. Few men can perform sexually if they are regularly humiliated.

Many men, self-conscious about the urgency of ejaculation, may adopt techniques to gain longer control. One ultimate result of this may be that he loses his erection, or fails to get one in the first place, because he is so concerned that his performance will not be long enough to please her.

Myth #12: All people are monogamous after marriage.

The divorce courts offer ample evidence that this myth is false. The danger in believing the myth is not so much that most people *are* tempted sometimes by outside diversions after marriage, but is in believing that the *marriage contract itself* guarantees monogamy and fidelity.

These are the myths that tend to break down or block out communication between partners about sex. Let's look at another potential obstacle.

Sex Role Identification

There is a difference between *sex roles* and *sexuality*, although the two are closely linked. Sex role has to do with the way men and women behave (or are expected to behave) in day-to-day activities. Sexuality refers to the expression of physical love. Today we see many evidences that old stereotyped sex roles are breaking down, that man, the bread-earner, aggressor, and woman, the passive homemaker, are beginning to blend together as people sharing lives and tasks. It is not beneath a woman to mow the lawn, repair the family car, or make reservations for social engagements. And many men are finding that they are not demeaned by changing diapers, running the vacuum, or cooking dinner.

This fracturing of rigid sex role definitions is a healthy trend. More women are getting in touch with their self-sufficient, independent, capable characteristics. More men are getting in touch with their nurturing, tender, dependent selves.

It is important to recognize that *we all have all of these sides* to our nature. It is entirely a matter of which side we choose to reveal or develop at any one time. Men are not innately logical and emotionally stoic and stable; women are not innately flighty and emotional. These are cultural myths fed to us since we were babies. It begins as soon as boy babies are dressed in blue and girls in pink. We do an injustice by segregating our little ones into the male or female roles with all the established stereotypes dragging along behind. It is a happy thing to see the changes now coming to pass in the flexibility of sex role differentiation. It is becoming permissible for either sex to engage in any activity. Little boys can play with dolls; little girls can play with bulldozers. Boys may be passive or aggressive and girls may be passive or aggressive—and both may behave differently at different times.

The important point relates to *your expectations* as you enter into a relationship. Define your role—not according to society's norms, but in *relation to your partner*—and be sure you understand each other.

In order to do this, two things are important:

1. Get in touch with your feelings *now*.
2. Do not feel that you must be consistent one way or the other all the time.

Moods and needs change for both of you, and the same is true of attitudes. If you recognize this going into a relationship, it will ease many problems as you go along.

For example, if you know your husband is a quiet individual who is not a "Mister fix-it" but rather enjoys reading, the arts, and stamp collecting, then you will not expect him to be an electrician or plumber or a great white hunter. If he knows you appreciate your own freedom to work outside the home and dislike housecleaning, he may be willing to do some of the household chores. He may even be a gourmet cook. The tenseness or relaxation with which you flow through varying roles together will have a profound effect upon relations in bed.

Above all, be honest with yourself and your partner about your feelings regarding sex roles. If you failed to do this before you began your relationship, do it now. Clear the air, and keep it cleared for the future. Getting in touch with your feeling about sex roles may not be easy, but it is essential.

In your workbook, write down your likes and dislikes concerning the sex role activities and attitudes you have, and compare this with what you really want to do and be. Then share your feelings with your partner. He may be amazed at the differences between his concept of your sex role and your attitudes toward it. If there are gaps between how you live and how you feel, begin to close them.

Problems and Expectations

Before we begin the exercises that will help you and your partner to improve your own sexual relations, it is important to go beyond the myths we have discussed to understand some of the more common areas of sexual expectation, misunderstanding, and disagreement.

Frequency of Sex

You may want sexual intercourse five times a week, but your wife does not. Or she may want it more frequently than you do. Do you sulk and fight about it, or hide your feelings and build up resentment?

One important rule is, *If you love and care, be available.* This is not the same as being a dull, passive receiver, because when either of you makes himself available, it's your choice to do so.

Be honest and don't pretend, but it's okay to be available for sex when your partner wants it. You, the man, can't force her to be turned on, but she can focus on the pleasantness of caresses, closeness, security, and touch. You, the woman, *do not fake orgasm.* You should be responsive, but do not pretend ecstasy. This confuses your husband by causing him to think he is giving you intense pleasure when he is not. If you are honest and direct in what you want and need, you and your partner will find ways to your orgasm when you need it.

Do *not* count the number of times you have sexual intercourse or orgasms. Pay attention to the intensity of feeling. Give clear signals and don't be coy. And remember, it is also okay for the man to say "no." He may not be able to get an erection or have an orgasm, but he can also enjoy pleasuring his partner and receiving pleasure in other ways. Accept the fact that he is not immune to problems any more than you are. And help him *not* to view any partial dysfunction or lack of enthusiasm for love-making at any particular time as a *failure*.

Quality of Sex

Both men and women should understand that sex doesn't begin at bedtime with five minutes of foreplay. Women treasure atmosphere and caresses that span a longer period of time. A continuous, warm feeling between the two of you, an atmosphere of intimacy, is good fertile ground for sex. Do not create an artificial atmosphere, but let her know in many ways that she is loved, and then sexual intercourse may develop spontaneously when you least expect it. Share your feelings and be open to each other.

Express What You Want

If you want to be held, tell him so. If you want her to caress you in a special way, tell her so. Often we are fearful of doing this because the request might repulse her (or him). Yet most of us want to please our partner, and appreciate being told how. Verbalize your feelings while this is happening so that your partner knows how it feels. He or she can thus share those feelings.

For women, it is important to stop playing seductive games. Be in touch with your feelings. If you say "no," be sure you mean "no." Love-making can be like eating. You might say, "I'm not hungry, but I'll prepare a meal for you because I enjoy your pleasure in eating." And it doesn't hurt to talk about the menu. Discuss the details (as you're making love), build on the excitement as it is generated—and don't hide in the dark.

Variety

You don't have hamburger and beans for dinner every night, so why should you make love the same way every night? Try a variety of postures and approaches. Try different positions and don't hesitate to ask for a new way of making love—either of you—if you'd like a change.

Much of the boredom of which both men and women complain comes from the fact that each knows exactly what move the other is going to make next and there are never any surprises. This is not to suggest that you try something you know to be repugnant to your partner, but don't assume that a variation of love-making is taboo until you check it out with him or her. If you have special desires, express them.

Using Sex as a Weapon

Some women, and men as well, withhold sex as a way of getting even for something a partner has done, or proffer sex as a bribe for something they want. Don't do this. It can kill love as well as the desire for sex.

Putting Conditions on Sex

A husband might say, "I'll make love to you if you'll do so-and-so." Such a thing might make the wife feel uncomfortable. A wife might demand, "I want you to lose weight before I'll make love to you," or "If you don't quit smoking, I won't go to bed with you."

Such things are the individual's choice, not yours to demand. This is similar to using sex as a weapon. If you *choose* to lose weight because you'll be more attractive to your partner, or if you *choose* to go braless because he likes it, that's quite another thing.

Orgasm

Virtually everyone presumes that a man achieves orgasm without difficulty. There are exceptions to this, of course. But now we're living in an age of great awareness—one might even say preoccupation—with the female orgasm.

If it is difficult for you, as a woman, to come through sexual intercourse alone, there are other ways to reach orgasm without denigrating or criticizing your partner.

You can do it yourself—either alone or in his presence. You are responsible for your own pleasure in reaching an orgasm.

Most women do not achieve orgasm at the same time as their partner. Be a bit selfish, both of you. Give yourself time. Focus upon your own pleasure and don't worry if you're too quick or too slow in getting there.

For the husband, be aware that your partner is responsible for *her own orgasm*. Certainly, you should do everything that you can to help her, but she should tell you how and it is her responsibility to reach that peak of pleasure, if she wishes to do so. If she refuses to let you use other caresses to make her come, that too is her choice. Sometimes a person may feel perfectly content after love-making even if orgasm is not achieved.

The nature and extent of caresses necessary to reach orgasm will be different at different times. For both of you, learn your body. Do not feel guilty in learning what pleases you. Indulge and enjoy.

As a woman may guide a man's hand to show him how to give her maximum pleasure, so a man may guide *her* hand in showing her how to help him get an erection, or reach an orgasm. Many women derive great pleasure from doing this.

And kiss any part of your partner's body that desires your kisses.

The key point is that we should be openly communicative and *help* our partner to do the things that give pleasure. But we are each responsible for our own pleasure. This should be your guide no matter how many years your relationship has endured.

The Male Erection

Many women ask, "What do I do when my partner cannot get an erection, or when he loses it?"

It is as common for men not to be able to engage instantly in sexual activity as it is for women. Treat your partner as a human being and not as a super performer. Loss of erection, therefore, should be treated as a normal occurrence. You may continue to stimulate your partner or ask him what he wants you to do. He might want simply to enjoy lying beside you and feeling your closeness and pleasure. He might want more stimulation, or he might want to discontinue sexual activity for the time being.

Any of these options is fine, just as it is acceptable for a woman not to want penetration or climax and still feel okay. It is extremely important for the man to accept his temporary loss of erection and still feel okay about himself. The more pressure we put on a man to achieve and maintain an erection, the more difficult it's going to be for him to do so.

For example, a woman of forty-five is married to a man of fifty-five. Up until now he has been the symbol of masculinity, living up to most of the male macho stereotype, but suddenly he has developed symptoms of partial impotence. Either he is unable to get an erection when she wants to make love, or his erection subsides before either of them reaches orgasm.

There may be many reasons for this, most of them

psychological. If the woman reacts with anger or ridicule, she can precipitate an anxiety syndrome on his part and, if she continues to respond to her mate in this fashion, she can be sure that he'll never again be able to make love to her satisfactorily.

If, instead, she is loving and supportive—and understands that *any* man can suffer temporary impotence at any time—then it is likely that his ability will recover. Also, as we have repeated, the erect penis is far from being the only tool we can use to deliver loving caresses. Our hands and mouth may be even better.

Premature Ejaculation

So-called premature ejaculation is a common problem among men.

As we have mentioned before, the woman should not be the judge of how long he should last, but if this condition exists occasionally, neither of you should worry about it. Concern and anxiety are the greatest enemies of male potency.

It is important for both partners to be fully aware that this is *not* exclusively the man's problem, and the woman must be supportive and motivated to resolve it with her partner. You must relax and change your attitude. The man must rid himself of anxiety, which in itself will improve his self-image and function, and the woman should take more responsibility for her pleasure.

In any case, premature is a relative concept. Ask yourself, "Premature in relation to what?" Must you wait with your orgasm until your partner comes in order not to be premature? What if it takes her an hour to achieve orgasm? Do you think that you have to "maintain" all this time in order not to be considered premature?

Various books on premature ejaculation define it in

terms of time spans. Some East Coast experts hold that a man needs to be able to hold his erection for five minutes in order to be normal. West Coast experts estimate about thirty seconds is normal. To them, less than thirty seconds constitutes premature ejaculation. Are there really such differences between West Coast potency and East Coast potency?

We mention this only to reassure you that premature ejaculation is a relative concept. Most probably, the cause and the cure is *in your mind*. You are okay. Nothing is the matter with you; nothing is wrong. If you can relax and remind yourself that sex is for pleasure and not for contest or performance, then premature ejaculation will disappear without any treatment.

If you have this problem, adopt the attitude that *you are not on stage performing.* You are the way *you* are, and your mate should accept you (as you should accept her) with your imperfections, weaknesses, and vulnerabilities. If it requires a prolonged time for her to reach orgasm, why isn't it okay for you to come in five minutes, if that's the way it works?

If your man has this problem, focus your attention on his humanness. Both of you need and deserve pleasure, but do not focus on the end results of sexual intercourse. Relax and enjoy what you have. Invent caresses to make up for what you don't have, and you can both overcome inadequacies. If you both fix your attitudes (and attitude often governs sexual adequacy), you will be able to overcome most sexual problems.

The key is love. Think of *loving* each other rather than *making* love to or for your partner.

The Affair

This is a difficult and delicate subject. If you are married—or living with someone in a less formal relationship—

what happens when you're attracted to someone else? The first thing to do about the subject is to discuss this frankly with your partner *before* the situation arises. Do it now, while you're in the process of working on your marriage.

It is almost inevitable that sometime during your marriage you will be attracted to someone else. Realize that it's okay to be aroused sexually by what you see, but this doesn't mean that you have to act on it. Some people try to deny their own feelings, but this leads to guilt and guilt may be transferred to resentment of your partner. That can lead to the dissolution of your marriage.

Many men and women fantasize about someone else when they are making love to each other. There is nothing wrong with this and, indeed, if both are secure in their love, they may be excited and stimulated by sharing each other's fantasies.

However, it is important that both of you decide what you will do if you're tempted to have an outside affair. If you have an opposite-sex friendship outside your marriage you are certain to share ideas and feelings and to touch that person. Sexual attraction grows naturally whether you're twenty years old or sixty.

Can your partner trust you not to indulge in sex with another person? Can you trust yourself? Will your marriage be able to stand an outside affair? Almost anyone can be swept away in the heat of a moment, but it is important to think about this in a calm moment and to clarify how you want to handle such a situation.

You may turn it off. You may just "let it happen." And you may pursue the love affair. Whichever way it goes, it is your *decision* and your *responsibility* to discuss it with your partner, preferably before you plunge into a love affair.

Let's presume, for example, that you decide to pursue an outside relationship. It's too beautiful to pass up. What happens then? More to the point, do you enter into the affair with *full awareness* of the consequences?

In most cases, if you asked your partner's permission to have sexual relations with another person, he or she would be hurt and say "no" emphatically. The fear of loss works that way and, of course, this leads to an impasse without logical solutions. You can't force your partner to change his or her attitudes, so if you decide to go ahead with the affair anyway, it might dissolve your marriage. In your mind, this outside affair might be essentially meaningless, just a passing passion, but you do not want to give up your marriage. If you persist in having an affair, you should realize that you're playing with fire. Know the penalty in advance, and don't delude yourself.

It is a rare couple that feels so secure in each other's love that they can give permission to each other for outside love adventures. A few are able to give their mate enough space to "do his (her) own thing," but most often the outside affair damages the original relationship to the point of no return, even when both partners are convinced that their commitment to each other is solid.

If you pursue outside affairs to substitute for your partner's failings, recognize that there are some basic faults in your marriage. The best course is usually to work on the marriage rather than to seek outside solutions for your unhappiness. If you substitute, you may find nothing but another unhappy situation.

Intimacy Self-Appraisal

Now that you have seen clearly some of the areas in which sexual frustrations and disagreements can exist, it is time to look more closely at your own relationship. The first step is to appraise your sexual attitudes. Use your workbook and write down how you value sexual relations with your partner:

Sex: Myth and Reality

1. Is it to express your love?
2. Is it to relieve your sexual urge?
3. Is it to bring yourself emotionally closer to your partner?
4. Is it to relieve anxiety?
5. Is it to patch up arguments?
6. Is it to just plain have fun?

You may add to the list. You also will discover that at different times you feel differently about sex relations and therefore behave differently with your partner. You ask for different things and you give in different ways.

In most marriages, sex and communication are common problem areas, and are closely related. The better the verbal and nonverbal communication between partners, the better the sexual relations, as a rule. Then there are some marriages in which almost everything is going wrong *except* sex. Such a marriage can last for a while, but not for long. Good sex alone is not enough to keep a troubled marriage together.

Ask yourself a few fundamental questions and compare your answers with your partner.

1. *What does sex mean to me?*
Make a list of descriptive words, in order of priority for you. For example, sex means to me: love, closeness, lust, fun, intimacy, sharing, openness, excitement, turn on, expression.

2. *What do you think sex means to your partner?*
Write the words you think your partner will write and the order in which you believe he or she would list them.

3. *In what areas are you very similar in terms of sexual wishes and needs?*

4. *In what areas are you very different?*
Compare notes and discuss them.

Here is an example of sexual differences:

Marlene needs a long period of foreplay to become aroused. She needs a romantic atmosphere and warm communication before sex. She also dislikes talking while making love.

Allen likes to surprise Marlene and make love quickly and spontaneously. He does not need verbal communication before sex, but he would like her to talk about her feelings while they're making love. He also wants Marlene to initiate sexual relations more often, and to be less inhibited in experimenting with sexual techniques.

Allen and Marlene have three basic choices:

1. To discuss their preferences and care enough to fulfill the other's needs. (In this option, you put your partner's needs ahead of your own.)
2. To bear their disappointment and frustration in silence. (This is a negative choice.)
3. Ask each other for pleasure, as *equals*. (Recognition of *equal* responsibility to give and receive pleasure can lead to a mutually satisfactory compromise. There is no self-sacrificing martyrdom here.)

Sexual Intimacy and Closeness

Some people can renew closeness through sexual intimacy. Sex for them *creates* new closeness. Others need to share feelings first through verbal expression in order to feel close and loving, and then to engage in sexual intercourse.

There is no one right way to enhance intimacy. Sex means different things to you at different times, and likewise to your spouse. Therefore, it's a good idea to check out your partner's mood each time you feel like making love. Listen. Be aware. And respond.

Examine your feelings as you begin. Do you feel loving and intimate? If you do, tell your partner. He or she will appreciate hearing how you feel.

Do you tell your partner clearly how you feel during sexual intercourse, or do you assume that he or she can guess? *Never expect your partner to guess.* Tell him what gives you pleasure. Guessing and presuming your partner's feelings reduces sexual excitement and feeling. Also, if you are just available to satisfy his needs at this moment, be sure he understands that you care enough to give pleasure, and enjoy the giving alone.

Love and feelings of closeness can be nourished. One way to increase these feelings is to *will* yourself to love. Love is a way of thinking, a decision, and a choice. Feeling "loving" is emotional, but it is also a decision each hour or each day. Here is an exercise to practice expressing positive feelings of love.

In your workbook, write a love letter to your partner pretending he is far away and you won't be seeing him for six months. Forget about the annoyances of everyday life and think positively about the good things you share, about your longing to be with him, to hold him, to love him. Describe how you would like to express your love and intimacy. Although your lover is not far away, this daily fantasy love letter can help you make the decision to view him as a special person. And your writing can become a self-fulfilling prophecy, especially if you share your letters with each other.

Intimacy and Empathy

Most people need to love. Staying in love within a committed relationship, such as marriage, requires a decision. It requires will power, the will to overlook small annoyances, to resolve fights as they occur, to retain the images which arouse and excite you, and above all to do things which please you and your partner. Focus on pleasing each other. Ask your partner what he likes. How can I create a mood in which both of us will be responsive to each other? What turns him on? What turns me on?

Intimacy requires that each partner understands the other's needs and feelings. *Intimacy demands empathy*.

- Do you express your empathy?
- Do you enjoy giving pleasure?
- Are you willing to learn and be guided by your partner in the ways you can increase his or her pleasure?

Sexual involvement requires the ability to express feelings both verbally and nonverbally. For some men it is easier to act out physically than to express themselves verbally. For some women it is easier to talk out their feelings and desires than to initiate physical intimacy. You need to merge the two abilities in order to communicate effectively about your sexual relationship.

Intimacy Exercises

The following exercises are important, and are designed to help you improve your intimate communication. You can achieve this goal only by setting aside a special time reserved for getting close to your partner. Use your workbook to clearly define your own wishes and feelings, some of which you may be sharing with your partner for the first time.

1. *Write a list of all the things that turn you on sexually*. Don't be embarrassed to detail each of the kinds of touch, caress, massage, word, hug, atmosphere, conversation that stimulates you. The important thing is to

tell *in detail* what you like. Some men and women are turned on by the use of earthy words for the sex act and organs. There is nothing wrong in this, of course, as long as it is a mutual turn on. After you and your partner each have written your list of sexual turn ons, then exchange lists, read them aloud and discuss them. Then, set aside time with your partner and *try all of them.*

2. *Determine a set time for you to be close to each other.* Take turns in expressing how you feel about yourself (your day at work, your moods) and then express your feelings toward your partner. Focus on positive statements and be honest. Look for something attractive in your partner, and focus on things that will please him or her. Express your sexual desires and fantasies toward each other. Then share how it felt to have this exchange.

3. *Set aside a time for body relaxation through touching, holding, massage, etc.* If you wish to massage one another, you may do it with or without clothes and with or without oils. Caring contact is the important element. If you are receiving the massage, focus on your own body. Let go of extraneous thoughts and worries. Block out other realities and focus on your physical pleasure. Guide your partner and teach him how to increase your pleasure. (Love-making thus can be taught by *you.*)

4. *Use all senses during love-making.* See what fragrance helps you to relax, to be aroused, or to release your inhibitions. You may choose to look at your body, your partner's nude body, or examine each other. You may have erotic pictures in your room, watch erotic movies, or do whatever excites you. Learn to smell your partner's distinctive odors, enjoy sounds of voice and breathing, and taste the very essence of your partner.

When you learn to love each other as equals, respecting each other's most intimate needs and desires, it is almost impossible *not* to have good physical relations.

Sex-Related Communication

This is an opportunity to discuss and hear each other's likes, dislikes, and preferences, and to understand your partner's sexual attitudes. Examine your own myths and beliefs about your sexuality and share this information with your partner.

Carry on a dialogue, take turns in talking and showing your partner how he or she can increase your sexual pleasure. Ask yourself if you can enjoy intimacy without expecting specific performance and an end result.

Get in touch with your real feelings about your sexual needs and your expectations from your partner. We read so much about how the new progressive man and woman *should* feel about sex that sometimes we lose touch with who we really are.

Don't worry about being labeled old-fashioned or puritanical. You are what you've been taught to be. Be honest with yourself. Do you both fully accept the statement that the man is not responsible for a woman's orgasm? If you do, this means you can relax while making love and focus on the pleasure of your own orgasm. Can you—the man—focus on your pleasure without feeling guilty, without feeling anxious about your wife? Can you—the woman—accept the statement that you are responsible for your own orgasm? If you do, then it means that you can reach orgasm without your partner, through self-pleasuring (masturbation). We should re-emphasize that there is nothing wrong in that.

You can choose to enjoy sexual intercourse without reaching a climax, or enjoy arousing your partner and, through his orgasm, feel close to him and satisfied. Be honest with yourself. In your workbook write all your feelings about your sexual response. Share it with your partner.

If your partner tells you that he or she enjoys and chooses to have sex without reaching orgasm, accept it. It is *not* a reflection of your lack of masculinity or femininity, nor does it indicate inadequacy. When giving pleasure, give only what is requested. Don't demand that your partner receive a gift that he or she does not desire.

The Female Orgasm

Although we have touched upon the female orgasm, it is important to explore the subject a little further to put this preoccupation into perspective.

First of all, recent research has established almost without question that the female orgasm is triggered through stimulation of the clitoris. For most women, the girth or length of a husband's penis is literally unimportant (except possibly as a visual turn on or turn off) because the tiny clitoral organ at the top of the vaginal entrance is the key to all orgasms.

And that leads to the issue of great expectation. Must a woman have an orgasm every time she makes love? Many women complain about their partner's insistence that each time they have sexual relations she experiences orgasm. This insistence and expectation cause many women to fake it.

A woman is not frigid even if she never achieves climax through intercourse. She can enjoy her sexuality and intimacy with her partner in many ways, and not desire to be orgasmic. Any woman who enjoys physical intimacy and sexual closeness is not frigid.

However, many women still feel that something is

wrong with them if they don't have orgasm, and that myth has destroyed many marriages. Examine your relationship in this regard. By changing your attitude—and the demands from yourself and your partner—you will have worked through a major obstacle to harmony.

For example, if you can convince your husband that he is not responsible for your pleasure and orgasm, he may become more relaxed and effective as a lover. Then, if you can concentrate on the pleasure, and not worry about whether you will climax, it is likely to come naturally. Give this time to work; it won't happen overnight if the two of you have already built habits that must be changed.

Problems to Resolve

How do you handle a situation in which you want sexual intercourse but your partner wants only physical closeness?

First, be honest and clear with each other. If one of you prefers physical closeness without intercourse, you can hold and touch each other, agreeing that sex is not to be imposed.

As an exercise, try to stay on the level of intimacy or distance that satisfies both of you each day for two weeks. Understand that feelings will change from one day to the next and neither partner should force his wishes upon the other. This exercise will build trust and help you to relax while you are in close, loving contact.

For the next two weeks, experiment by taking turns in doing for your partner what he or she requests. If your spouse asks for closeness that you don't enjoy, tell him (her) and substitute another form of pleasure which *both* of you will enjoy. This exercise will help you accept the idea of mutual pleasuring, and demonstrate your freedom to express your likes and dislikes. A deep, intimate relationship can grow only through deep communication.

Intimacy: Re-evaluation Exercises

A. Think back to how it was in the beginning of your relationship. Ask each other the following questions:

1. What attracted you to me?
2. What did you feel when we first met?

Go back in memory to when you met, or the first time you experienced the special feeling of falling in love. Write down the memories in your journal. Relive the experience in fantasy and share it with your partner.

B. Recall and write down the *good times* in your life together. Relive the specially intimate moments you have shared (not sexual relations). Intimacy includes the joy of dating, closeness on a vacation, the thrill of seeing your child take his first step, etc. You did have moments of closeness and intimacy, even if perhaps those moments have lately become fewer and farther between.

C. What is missing now? How are things different? Do we want to bring this positive feeling of intimacy back to life? Take time out, separately, to think about these questions. Try to originate three suggestions as to how to bring back the missing element in your relationship. Share these suggestions—and *try* them.

D. Perhaps one of you feels that the sexual relationship is "unsatisfying." Rather than expressing yourself so generally, try being more specific:

1. I need more expression of affection.
2. I need more caresses or more verbal exchange.
3. I want to express my affection for you spontaneously, at any time or place, not just when we're alone.

Avoid expressing what you need in a destructive way by accusing the other person of fault, such as not caring, being selfish, or being an inadequate lover.

The charge of inadequacy, for example, is loaded. Everything is relative but measurements of adequacy and inadequacy are totally subjective. Most people have a fantasy of how a good lover should behave. They then relate to their partner according to their expectations. If you do not relate your expectations frequently and freely discuss them with your partner, you might not get what you need from your mate. You may conclude that someone else could fulfill your fantasies. But it is possible that no one could, and you may, in fact, have everything you need within your own pasture. If you're not getting it, ask for it. You may have to ask for it more than once and in more than one way. Assert your need and express its intensity.

Usually, when we want something not associated with sex, we ask for it matter-of-factly. In sexual communication, however, many people are inhibited and give nonverbal cues rather than telling what they want. It is important to develop your ability to express your likes, dislikes, wishes, and needs. Nonverbal hints often are missed or misinterpreted. Simple words can clarify an unclear message.

E. List in your workbook all the words that express your moods and needs in a sexual relationship. Also list the words by which you think of the sexual organs and the sexual experience. Start with the ones simple for you, and then try others which you may find inhibiting or uncomfortable.

Remember that no word is evil or forbidden in itself. Which of these words arouses you? Which ones are neutral or uncomfortable? Share your words and your feelings about them with your partner. You may be surprised at how much this exercise may illuminate some of your partner's sexual behavior.

F. Good sex depends on the degree to which you enjoy giving pleasure to your partner. Write a list of how many ways your partner can please you, and in how many ways you enjoy pleasing him or her. Examples might be massaging, bathing together, kissing, hugging, sucking, holding, sharing feelings, etc. Share your answers *in detail* with your partner.

Touch for touch's sake. We should realize that not all touching must lead to sexual intercourse. Touch can be purely sensual, pleasant for its own sake, or sexual in nature. If a partner's touch habitually leads to sexual encounter, then that feeling will be invoked whenever we are touched. However, if we give ourselves the option that touch may or may not lead to sexual intercourse, then we allow ourselves a much wider range of feelings.

A good way to rediscover the simple pleasure of touch is through massage. Take turns in massaging one another as you did in the intimacy exercise earlier. Share your feelings during and after. Also, be aware if you feel the need to reciprocate immediately after you have been massaged. In our culture, we have been taught to return a favor quickly. We can get carried away, however, in our need to reciprocate immediately. Gerald Smith and Alice Phillips, in their book *Me, You and Us,* wrote:

> Some people have great difficulty in being passive

receivers only. They have to reciprocate at the same time. They cannot conceive of simply soaking up an experience. . . . People who can receive without reciprocating are also usually able to give without expecting to be paid back.

Practice receiving pleasure from your partner and learning to be comfortable with it.

G. Instant feedback. In order to enrich your sexual relations, you and your partner must maintain open and honest communication. We cannot overemphasize this. Always give feedback without withholding any feelings. Positive feedback is just as important as a request for a different touch or stroke.

You may say, "That feels relaxing," or "That feels good," or "Keep doing just what you're doing." At the same time, don't feel obligated to say anything. Your body language may be loud enough. Your pleasure (or lack of it) may be obvious to your partner, but it is your responsibility to let him know what pleases you and what does not. Acknowledge, encourage, and compliment your partner when he is giving you pleasure.

Boredom

One of the more common complaints among couples is that they are bored with the habitual ways they make love. When you are bored, tell your partner—not in an accusing way, but in a way that will encourage change. Together you can find new ways to enhance your sexual relations. Change of scenery, time, days, engaging in fantasy, all these can be healthy and refreshing. Role playing—pretending you are someone else in a different place, with different clothes and a different image—can be exciting. Taking vacations without the children can do wonders.

There are many ways to combat boredom in a close relationship, but it takes initiative, imagination, and a willingness by both partners to enrich and enhance their intimate life.

> A. Using your workbook, list five situations in which you experience boredom in your marriage, either with your partner or when alone.
> B. List five things you like to do alone to help you combat boredom.
> C. List five things you would like to do with your partner to combat boredom and enliven your marriage.
> D. Once a week, try to re-evaluate your sexual feelings toward your partner. If you feel distant, bored, or turned off, again write a list of things that you want to do for yourself and with your partner to revitalize your marriage.

You are the only one responsible for your state of boredom. Therefore, you are responsible for getting yourself out of it. It requires a new decision and a change in behavior, but if you decide you don't want to be bored, you will find ways to change your situation.

As you have seen, sex can either be a beautiful experience or a negative one. It depends upon how you want it to be and how you go about getting what you want. Of utmost importance is clearly asking for what you need. Communicate with your partner. If you are in a loving union, and ask for what you want, barring any extraordinary physiological impairment, you should be able to have a healthy and growing sexual relationship together.

7
Values and Meaning

Gene pushed his chair back from the breakfast table and put on his coat.

"Wish me luck," he said, "today's the day we come to grips with the problem of Ralph."

Doris knew what he meant. They had talked about it before, but she was troubled.

"Are you sure you want to do that?" she asked.

Gene paused, an expression of annoyance on his face.

"Yes, I'm sure," he said at last. "You know I need that job and Ralph should have been retired years ago. I know the mistake he made that lost that big contract six months ago, and I'm going to tell the president."

"I wish you wouldn't do it," Doris said. "I don't think it's right."

Now she knew she had made her husband angry and she didn't want to send him off to work that way. Yet, she also knew he was not basically an avaricious person. Somehow his values had changed since he started climbing up the hierarchy of his corporation.

"It's really for Ralph's own good," Gene said defensively. "His retirement checks will be adequate, and besides, I think his health has been slipping lately. He needs a rest."

"That may be true," Doris answered, "but I still don't like the feeling that you're the one who's going to turn the knife."

"All right!" He was really angry now. "Then suppose *you* tell me how to get that promotion. You like this house, don't you, and the other good things my paycheck brings home?"

"Yes, you know I do," Doris said wearily. "But I guess I don't value those things as much as you do."

Gene left without kissing her goodbye.

Value

Doris used one of the key words in life. A conflict in *values* can be one of the basic sources of marital difficulties. A value can be defined as a principle by which we lead our lives. Our lives contain *meaning* in proportion to our ability to live according to our principles, while achieving the things we value most.

Life is an uninterrupted search for meaning; meaning which will help one measure the significance of his or her role in the world in relation to him(her)self and other people. We hear such statements as, "My life has no meaning anymore," or "My relationship with John is very meaningful." The word "meaning" in fact, has attained a fashionable buzz-word status in current society, and its overuse may obscure what we are talking about.

In general, if you feel good about what you are doing, if life is interesting, exciting, ethical, and fulfilling, it has meaning. If none of these elements exists, your life has little meaning. You do not feel good about what you are doing (or what is being done to you), and much discomfort can arise from conflict with a partner whose values do not match yours.

There is a close relationship between your values and whether or not your life seems to have meaning. But meaning is certainly not dependent upon being married or single. Peter Koestenbaum, in his book *Existential Sexuality; Choosing to Love,* talks about the search for meaning and marriage, and separates the issues as follows:

1. Love, sex, marriage, family, and meaning are independent variables.
2. A person can choose to find meaning in life *without* marriage.
3. A person can choose to find meaning in life *through* marriage.
4. A person can choose to find meaning in life *in spite of marriage*.
5. A person can choose to find meaning in life by *reforming* his or her marriage.

Thus, meaning for any individual can be found in many ways. Marriage relations can add meaning to life, but you can also find your meaning in spite of an unfulfilled marriage. Or, you can change the quality of your relationship so that you can bring meaning to your life either alone or as part of a couple.

Value Identification

Since meaning is so closely associated with values, this is a good time to identify your values, some of which may have changed, or even have been forgotten since your last conscious examination. We make dozens of value judg-

Values and Meaning

ments and decisions in the course of a day, and often we are not conscious of doing so.

For example, should I vacuum the house today, because my husband enjoys a clean house, or should I put off doing it because I'd prefer to go shopping even though he's worried about bills? The decision may not be a big one, but it indicates the value (in your mind) of a clean house versus the pleasure of shopping. Or, for the husband, do I go out and play poker with the boys tonight, or do I spend the evening with my wife?

These two simple value decisions—small as they are in themselves—imply possible conflict with a spouse. The husband likes to find a clean house when he comes home and is concerned with how his wife spends their money. For her part, she may resent his time with the boys because evenings after work are the only occasions when she and her husband can be together.

Other small value decisions (which may not affect a partner directly) include such things as:

Do you give yourself enough time before work for a good, nourishing breakfast, or do you starve yourself until lunch because you prefer to linger in bed those extra minutes?

Do you value your body by setting aside time each day for exercise—such as walking, jogging, or racquet ball —or do you ignore your body by sitting in front of a desk all day and in front of the television all evening?

Most of us form habit patterns built upon our values, and thus some of our decisions are unconscious. In this case, how do you identify your values specifically and, more important, how do you identify those areas in which your values conflict with your partner's?

One way is for each of you to sit down alone and check out how you feel about different life issues, and then compare your answers. This may be most revealing. Do this in your workbook so that you have a continuing record of where you've been and where you're going. Chances are, some of your earlier values will have changed from what you thought they were, and some of the changes may have resulted from interactions with your partner. The following questions may prompt such an examination:

Work

- What do I want professionally for myself?
- One year from now?
- Three years from now?
- Five years from now?
- Is professional advancement the most important thing in my life?
- Am I in the right profession?

Money

- To be happy, is it important for me to have a lot of money?
- What is a lot of money to me?
- What is a moderate amount?
- What is the subsistence level?
- On what do I want to spend my money?

Time

- Is it important to me to have a lot of time to myself?
- Would I rather do things by myself?
- Would I rather do things with my spouse?
- How do I like to spend my leisure time?

Children

- Is it important to my happiness to have children?
- If so, how many?
- How would this affect my other goals regarding work, money, time, etc.?

Values and Meaning

- If I already have children, how is it affecting my other life values?
- Am I against having children at all?
- Do I believe in birth control?
- Abortion?

Child Rearing

- Do I believe in leniency with children?
- Strictness?
- Do I need more consistency in this area between me and my spouse?

Friends

- Do I need many friends outside my marriage relationship?
- Do I want to see my friends alone all the time?
- With my spouse sometimes?
- With my spouse included all the time?

Home

- Do I want a home in the woods, even at the expense of a long commute to work and leisure?
- Would I prefer a home in the city with its hustle and bustle?
- Do I want to furnish my home richly?
- Or furnish it moderately, with more money left to spend for other things?
- Do I insist on immaculate cleanliness?
- Or do I let the house take care of itself because other things are more important?

Entertainment

- Do I prefer quiet evenings at home with a book or TV?

- Dinner and dancing dates with my spouse?
- Spectator sports?
- Theater and movies?
- Music concerts and ballet?
- Fishing, golf, or similar sports?
- Camping in the woods?
- World travel?
- Do I enjoy sharing these things with my spouse?

You may add other topics that are important to you. Let your mind roam. You probably will find areas in which your values match your partner's quite closely—after all, certain such similarities were involved in your choice of a mate. However, we change with time and this inventory of values will intensify your awareness of what changes have taken place.

After you've each sorted out your values and written them down, get together and compare your responses. You probably had discussions like this when you were dating before marriage, but it is a good idea to check out periodically with each other where you stand on certain issues. How often you do this is up to you—whatever is comfortable. But if you do it every year or two, it will help you understand your partner's position and avoid situations in which small conflicts become big ones.

For example, Susan and Ralph had difficulty agreeing on their values and priorities in the use of leisure time. Bill enjoyed sports and spent his free time outdoors. Susan enjoyed reading and listening to classical music. As a result, they spent little time together and grew apart.

Each resented the other's position but, rather than letting the resentment grow, they discussed the situation and discovered that each had a higher priority than their hobbies —both wanted to be together. After they understood this, it became less difficult to negotiate how they would spend the time together. They used good communication and negotiating skills to satisfactorily live with each other's values.

Dave and Debbie disagreed on the value of friends. Debbie needed other people, cherished her friendships, and enjoyed social gatherings. Dave did not trust people, was bored at parties, and did not have the patience to mix with people. He was also a workaholic. He resented coming home from a busy day at the office, only to be told they were expected to go out for an evening with friends.

Debbie explained to Dave how important friends were in her life, and that she needed them for listening and support. Dave, in turn, told her how he had been disappointed by friends in the past. In the place of friends, he had found that work gave him a sense of accomplishment, success, and the reward of high income. He could rely upon himself and did not see the need to associate with other people.

By sharing and clarifying what was important, Dave and Debbie were able to pursue their valued activities with a deeper understanding of each other.

The *first* step was to share what was important to both of them.

The *second* was to reach a better understanding of *why* it was important.

The *third* step was to determine how each of them could partially satisfy the other partner's needs and desires.

The *fourth* and *final* step was compromise.

Debbie offered to introduce Dave to some of her best friends. As he got to know them better, he found he could like and respect them. In return, Debbie gave Dave more support and recognition for his work achievements. Not too surprisingly, as Debbie paid more attention to his needs, goals, and aspirations, Dave found that he needed less such satisfaction from immersion in his work. And the two of them found even more time for pleasant activities together.

The Valuing Process

Before we delve more deeply into questions of conflicting values—and your options when values are contrary—it is important to know whether what you have in mind is a true value or a passing fancy or whim. Simon, Howe, and Kirschenbaum, in their book *Values Clarification,* refer to seven processes (developed by Louis Raths) in recognizing a value. To see if your position reflects a serious value, ask yourself the following questions (write each issue, and your answers, in your workbook):

1. Are you *proud of* (do you prize or cherish) your position?
2. Have you *publicly affirmed* your position?
3. Have you chosen your position from *alternatives?*
4. Have you chosen your position after *thoughtful consideration* of the pros and cons and the consequences?
5. Have you chosen your position *freely?*
6. Have you *acted* on or done anything about your beliefs?
7. Have you acted with *repetition,* a pattern of consistency, on this issue?

Let's try these seven questions on an example:

Peg and Art have been married for five years. Peg does not like obesity or fat people, but after marriage she has become careless and gradually gained thirty pounds.

Peg had never suffered a weight problem before, so she is not unduly concerned. However, she does not enjoy huffing and puffing up a stairway, or feeling less sexy, or Art's occasional jokes about her "love handles." Art insists that he is not disturbed by her added weight ("There's more to love!"), but Peg is concerned that it might affect their relationship.

She decided to join a class in which behavior modification techniques are used to stress change in eating habits and becoming aware of, and implementing, these changes. She is now in the fifth week of classes and excited over the prospect of making permanent change.

Is this desire to lose thirty pounds a goal based upon genuine value, or something she is likely to give up in a few weeks? Let's see if she fulfills the seven criteria:

1. Yes, she is pleased to reach the decision to lose weight.
2. She has told her husband and friends about her decision.
3. She has chosen to lose weight over the alternatives of staying at her present weight or gaining more.
4. Although eating a lot of her favorite foods is pleasant momentarily, the bloated feeling and lack of control she feels afterward are not pleasant. To feel more confident and good about herself would be positive consequences if Peg loses weight.
5. Peg chose to lose weight because she wasn't feeling good physically, and because she didn't like the way she looked. Art's subtle comments may have influenced her, but it was Peg's dissatisfaction with herself that was the main determining factor.
6. Peg acted on her desire to lose weight by joining a weekly group which is teaching her a sensible, permanent way to do it.
7. Peg has gone to class for five weeks so far and is excited about the remaining seven weeks in the course. She is practicing what she has learned and is reshaping her habits on a daily basis.

As you identify your own values, you may test each of them against these seven questions. If the value has caused you to set a goal, the seven steps will probably assist you in reaching that goal because it has been clearly defined for you. In order to get what we want out of life, we must know what it is we want. We can't approach a goal unless we know what it is! You might find that a value which is in conflict with your mate is, in actuality, not that important to you anymore.

Different Values

When you and your partner went over the previous value questions regarding work, money, time, children, and other added items, you probably discovered several areas in which your values diverge appreciably. What do you do about it?

You have several options:

1. You can each do what you wish and disregard the validity of the other person's values. You can live in your own separate worlds. However, if you do that, what is your basis for marriage?

2. You can go along with what your partner wants to do this time, with the provision that he'll do what you want to do next time. For example, you both share the priority that you want to be together tonight. Frank wants to go to a movie, but Barbara wants to go dancing. They might agree to go to a movie tonight and next time to go dancing, or vice versa.

3. You might find a third alternative which, although not your first choice, is acceptable to both of you. Frank is sure he doesn't want to go dancing and Barbara really does not want to sit and watch a film. They finally agree on the idea of joining another couple to play bridge or backgammon. This option is amenable to both of them.

4. Over the long term, there is a fourth possible choice—helping one or both to change values so that their

Values and Meaning

wishes may be more in harmony with each other. This gets back to discovering the "why" of a value decision. Frank does not like dancing because he considers himself a lousy dancer and fears embarrassment on the dance floor. Barbara does not like movies because her eyes are weak and the flickering images give her a headache. If Frank took a few dancing lessons, he might learn to love dancing. Barbara might then get "into" films a bit to share Frank's enjoyment of them.

Understanding and communication both to yourself and your partner are the basic factors. Some people neither know what they really value nor ever tell their partners what they want or what they believe. Once this information is shared and understood, then there is room for compromise rather than conflict.

When you are part of a couple, you cannot expect to live a life without compromise. Learning the art of compromise can also be fun. It takes creativity and imagination. Fortunately, most value decisions are not purely black or white, and it is important to remember that in almost all situations there really is room for compromise, if you *want* to. If you don't want to compromise, then you won't. You'll reach a stalemate. *Wanting* to find a compromise is the opening key.

As you work through values and meaning, and come to understand your partner's positions, you will find that some areas of conflict are more serious than others. Also there are areas wherein alternate choices and compromise are difficult to find. Two of these, for example, involve whether or not to have children, and a marriage in which the partners profess widely divergent religious beliefs. Such major questions as these certainly should be talked out and agreed upon in some fashion during the courtship process. However, so many modern relationships follow hasty courtships that there is not enough time to fully communicate on all the important issues with each other, or resolve major questions that are surefire marriage breakers.

Even so, such problems can be approached and resolved if the partners are serious in wishing to do so. The best procedure is to resolve minor value conflicts first, weeding out the relatively easy problem areas so that a climate of compromise and understanding is already established before you tackle the big ones.

Setting Priorities

It is important to identify and get in touch with those things which really mean a lot to us—values we are not willing to compromise or relinquish. At the same time, we can readily identify those values upon which we are more flexible, less adamant.

Following are some statements for you to answer. Do this exercise in your workbook separately, and then get together to compare notes. First, get in touch with how you feel about the contents of the statement. If you're adamant about it—unwilling to bend or change—put an "**A**" to the left of the numeral. If you're flexible about it, put an "**F**" to the left of the numeral. Then rank these in order of importance to you—the highest number one, the next number two, etc.—by noting in the margin on the right of your paper.

Work on the most flexible conflict first. Then work up to those both or either partners feels most adamant about.

1. It's imperative that the house always be clean and in good order. I cannot stand dust, dirt, or clutter.
2. I must have some time to myself every week. I cannot stand to be a twosome all the time.

Values and Meaning

3. I want to attend at least one concert, opera, or ballet a month.

4. I must have time to bring work home or do graduate work without being nagged or feeling guilty about it.

5. I want to have moderately free rein on money without having to account for every penny I spend.

6. I want to contribute to all major decisions. I don't want to be told what we'll be doing. I don't want you to come home one night in a shiny, new car and tell me this is the new "family" car.

7. I want to have my own set of friends in addition to our mutual friends.

8. I want to have opposite-sex *platonic* friends.

9. I want to get away on a mini-vacation (a long weekend) at least once every three months. I need a change of scenery now and then.

10. I want all household, yard work, and car maintenance duties shared on a 50-50 basis.

Getting What You Want

Other people—even our intimate partner—cannot see what is going on inside our head. Sometimes we just have to ask bluntly for what we want.

This takes courage because it involves the risk that the other person may say, "No, I don't want to do that for you." You then have the option of being demoralized and never asking again for what you want, or of shifting and asking another person for what you want. Keep in mind, though, that *we can never have all of what we want at all times.* There is some frustration and disappointment in store for everyone. However, the sting and continuing pain of frustration and disappointment may be eased or even eliminated if you let your partner know how you feel about many things, as in the following exercise.

Fill in the following statements (in your workbook) and then share your responses with your partner. We've listed some examples as a guide, but let these statements reflect your true feelings about values and meaning in *your* relationship.

1. I love it when my spouse _____.
(Example: Leaves notes scattered around the house thanking me for something I've done for him or her, and telling me how much he or she loves me.)
2. I need my spouse to show me more _____.
(Examples: Respect; Attention; Affection.)
3. I hate it when my spouse _____.
(Examples: Leaves dirty dishes in the sink; Forgets car tools in unsafe places; Leaves a ring around the tub.)
4. I don't like it when my spouse teases me about ____.
(Examples: My weight; My cooking ability; My occasional disorganization; My sloppiness in dress and appearance around the house.)
5. I want my spouse to _____.
(Examples: Share his feelings with me more; Get into the habit of building me up rather than knocking me down; Listen to me more.)

Again, you may add more items and categories to this list, keeping in mind that we are trying to open communication channels. The exercise might help steer you to a specific value area that follows. The important thing to remember is that we are opening communication channels, clarifying values, setting priorities, and always negotiating.

8
The Use of Time

Except for the constraints of getting to work on time or turning on a favorite TV program, most of us pay little attention to the ways we use time, which may well be the most precious commodity in our lives.

Almost everyone wastes time now and then—which is our choice if it does not involve someone else's happiness. And it is not always bad to waste time. It is not necessary to engage in a continual frenzy of work or other activity, but it is important to find out if we are cheating ourselves and our mates of time that could be used more productively than the way we are now using it. Time gets away from us because we do not plan, or we fail to follow our plans. We use time carelessly, and only the leftover moments (usually just before falling asleep at night) are saved to share with our partners.

It is astonishing how many complaints we hear from married couples that concern the use of time:

- He is never on time. Dinner is ready and he's nowhere to be found.
- She has all day to clean the house and yet when I come home it's a mess. She wastes her time.
- She is never dressed and ready on time when we're going out. This spoils my evening. I hate to be late and I hate to rush. Why can't she be more prompt and considerate?
- He spends his weekends playing golf and never leaves time for me and the children. It feels like we're not important in his life.
- He never has time to sit and talk to me. Something more urgent always seems to take precedence. I don't like being second banana.

In light of such complaints, time is obviously a factor which can be used as an excuse for something else—perhaps for a wish to avoid closeness and intimacy. This is often true of the spouse who works at the office all day and then attends meetings almost every night, or one who works hard housecleaning all day and then is too tired for intimacy with his or her partner at night.

Time is valued, managed, and utilized in different ways by different people. What one person considers a waste of time, another may see as a valuable use. What is quality time (prime time) for one person might be viewed as procrastination by another.

For example, a wife who is concerned about the completion of odd jobs and repairs around the house would be irritated by the time her husband spends with his stamp collection, not realizing that he needs this time to relax from his job and refresh his spirit. Likewise, a husband might be angry if he came home to find his wife in front of the TV set while a sink-full of dirty dishes remained to be washed from breakfast. He might not understand that she turned to the television out of desperation to break the endless chain of boredom in doing housework.

The Use of Time

In order to resolve conflicts over time issues, you first must establish some information about yourself:
- How do you spend your time?
- What is important to you in life?
- What are the things you want to accomplish?
- What are the things you wish to experience?
- How do *you* manage and control your time?
- How do you set priorities (if you do at all), and how do you resolve your problems concerning time with your partner and time alone?

Weekly Time Log

Let's look at how you spend a typical week in your life, breaking it down into daily and hourly activities.

Record for a week all your activities *alone,* your activities together as a *couple,* and your activities as a *family.* Place the letter "**A**" beside the activities alone, "**C**" next to couple activities, and "**F**" beside family activities.

In another column on the page, designate those things you did because you enjoyed them, and those you did because it was your duty or you thought you *should* do them. Note an "**E**" for enjoyment and an "**S**" for should.

Make up seven pages in your workbook, one for each day of the week, and keep your record separate from your partner's. Make your own list following the example on page 158.

Your list and your partner's certainly will not match this one in all respects. The important point is to account for each hour in the day. Also, where you have marked **E** for enjoyment, you might mark on a scale of one to ten *how much* you enjoyed these activities.

At the end of the week compare your time log with your partner's. Discuss how many things you did—and how much time was spent—alone, together, or with the entire family. Also compare how many things you did because

Hour	Day and Activity	Alone A Couple C Family F	Enjoyed E Should S
	Monday		
7 A.M.	Prepared breakfast and ate	F	S
8	Cleaned house	A	S
9	Read a book	A	E
10	Shopped for groceries	A	S
11:30	Prepared lunch	A	S
Noon	Lunch with kids	F	E
1 P.M.	Telephoned friends	A	E
3	Talked with son	F	E
4	Answered letters	A	E
5	Prepared dinner	A	S & E
6	Dinner time	F	E
7	Discussed day's activities	C	E
8	Helped with homework	F	S
9	Relaxed before retiring	C	E
10	Went to bed and made love	C	E

you felt they were a duty. These logs will help each of you to see exactly how you spend your time.

Did you find changes you would like to make, such as spending more time together as a family? Do you spend too many hours on the "shoulds"? Are some of the Es on your list Ss for your partner? Would it improve your life to work more enjoyable activities into your schedule, or to revise some, such as reducing TV time in order to talk or play games with your partner or children? By becoming aware of how you spend your time, you probably will become more conscientious in using it well. You may be able to devise ways to make better use of time (in terms of what is important to you and your family) and thus have more time for the things of high priority.

By now it should be apparent that a study of your and your partner's time-use habits can add greatly to the day-to-day meaning in your marriage. Now you should begin working in those areas where conflicts occur between you over the use of time.

The Use of Time

Identifying Problem Areas

Recognize again that it is virtually impossible for two people in an intimate relationship to go through life without occasional or frequent conflicts about the use of time, as in other areas of your marriage. What problem areas exist in your relationship where time management is a factor? What things would you like to change? What things are you unwilling to change? Use "I" statements to express some of the changes you would like. For instance:

- I would like to go away with my partner once a month *without* the children.
- I would like to have a fixed time for family dinner.
- I would like to have time every day to share the day's happenings with my partner.
- I would like to spend some prime time (time when I'm most energetic and alert) on myself every day.
- I would like to spend some prime time alone with my partner every day.

After each of you has written your statements alone, compare them and discuss how you can fulfill your time needs while also considering your partner's needs. This exercise can help you identify those parts of your day and evening in which you use time habitually without realizing the effect it may be having upon your partner.

Don likes to take at least forty-five minutes over breakfast to digest the morning newspaper. Helen is unable to do this because she is busy getting his breakfast and preparing school lunches for the children.

Helen does her reading in the evening, in what she calls her "quiet time." It is immediately after dinner when her family has been fed and is comfortable. At that time, she takes an hour to read the evening paper and study the advertisements to make shopping plans.

Thus, between the two of them, two hours a day are

expended reading the papers *alone*. Helen resents her husband's lack of communication with her in the morning before he goes to work, and Don dislikes Helen's seclusion with the paper in the evening. A discussion of this situation led to several mutually pleasing resolutions.

1. Either one or both could postpone reading the paper to another time, or Don could get up an hour earlier in the morning if the paper is that important to him.
2. Both could spend *less time* reading the paper. Both Don and Helen agree that few news stories interest them deeply each day. The remainder of the paper could be scanned quickly.
3. It might be pleasant to discuss news items of mutual interest while they are reading. This could add depth and meaning to breakfast and after-dinner conversation.

A fourth outcome of Don and Helen's time discussion might be a new understanding that each feels that newspaper reading is the most pleasurable and valuable use of those particular times of the day. This way they could *give* this alone time to each other without feeling that the time was stolen from either of them.

Time Alone

We all need space and time to be alone. We need quiet, nondemanding time to think, create, read, enjoy, and procrastinate. Can you express this need without giving a signal that you're distinterested in, or rejecting, your partner? Try tactful assertive statements, such as:
- Today was really a killer at the office. I'd like to have a glass of wine and soak in the tub for half an

The Use of Time

hour and *then* share our day's experiences with each other.
- I played chauffeur all day and the phone never stopped ringing. I'd like to go into the study for an hour in absolute silence. Then we can have dinner.
- I had so many customer complaints today that I've got to be by myself for a while. I feel that if you just look at me cross-eyed, I'll hit the ceiling or you, or both! And I don't want to do that.

Leveling with your partner and saying precisely how you feel can do wonders in avoiding conflict and blowups. Most of us are more liable to lose our temper at the end of a day's work when we are tired and our energy level is low. It is therefore important to take care of your needs in a candid but tactful way at this crucial time of day.

Share with your partner how it felt when he or she expressed a need to spend time alone. If it felt like a rejection, is there another way it could be said so that you wouldn't feel that way, or is it necessary for you to adjust your attitude? Do you think it will always feel like a rejection if your partner expresses a need to be alone? If so, you need to rethink the rhythm of marriage, the natural cyclic flow of being together and apart that is necessary if a long-term relationship is to work. It is a mistake to grasp jealously and demand closeness when your partner needs time alone for a while.

Time Together

Select a page in your workbook and divide it into three columns labeled: (1) Outside the Home, (2) At Home, and (3) On Vacation. Now list the things you enjoy doing together, for example:

Outside the Home	At Home	On Vacation
Going to movies	Talking to each other	Visiting the city
Attending a concert	Listening to music	Touring Europe
Hearing a lecture	Reading aloud to one another	Taking a cruise
Visiting friends		Staying at a resort
Going out to dinner	Playing with the kids	Backpacking
Camping out	Gardening, painting, puttering	Room service
Hiking, swimming, tennis, etc.		

As you can see, certain pleasures are dependent upon both time and money (such as vacations). These activities involve budgeting your time and money. (The latter will be discussed in the following chapter.) If you budget one without solving the other, you will not be able to accomplish your goal.

Experiment with scheduling some activities in advance. Get season tickets to plays or concerts, or plan some house parties. Obviously, you need to check and see how all of this fits your partner's time schedule as well as your own. Social planning should always be a joint effort. If you find that you've scheduled too many activities (such as club meetings), cancel some of them or reduce the number for next month. This programing of time requires experimentation to discover the number and kinds of activities that are most comfortable for your partner and yourself, and assures your spending prime time together. Above all, leave time for spontaneous, nonplanned activities.

Creative Procrastination

Most of the time we think of procrastination as being wrong or negative—we have something we want to accomplish but keep putting it off. It may be negative if we make a habit of it. However, there are times when procrastination can serve a useful purpose.

The Use of Time

For instance, Patricia wanted to spend the day at the museum and local art galleries, but she also had a school assignment which had to be finished. She did not feel like tackling the project, nor did she feel she could afford the whole day away from it.

Pat decided to compromise with herself. Instead of going to the museum, she took a long walk, putting thoughts of the school assignment behind her, and she enjoyed it. She returned from the walk invigorated and with a fresh attitude that enabled her to work more effectively on the assignment.

It is important that we get away from feeling guilty all the time when we find ourselves procrastinating. There are times when this really is the most important thing to do. You can change your attitude toward procrastination by allowing *yourself* to decide the most important things you wish to accomplish each day. Alan Lakein, in his book *How to Get Control of Your Time and Your Life,* suggests you make up a "to do" list every day in an order of priority. Complete your number one priority before you spend time on numbers two, three, and so forth, and learn to recognize if and when you allow procrastination to work against you. There are many times when just "sitting and thinking" can help you to reach a faster and better way to do a job or solve a problem. And sometimes everything will work better if you just stop and take a short nap after lunch. This can sharpen your wits for better use of the rest of the time in the day.

Time for Intimacy

Many people assume that intimacy just happens, that it is not necessary to *make* time for it. This may be true early in a relationship, when you're both preoccupied with intimate touch, but many marriages gradually come unglued simply because the partners did not set a high priority on time for closeness with each other.

It is true that spontaneity is a vital ingredient of intimate relations. However, if you don't leave enough time and you start relating near midnight or ten minutes before you leave for work in the morning, it can be unsatisfying and frustrating to your partner. You may set up an atmosphere of resentment and miss many opportunities for closeness by just trying to squeeze time in here and there.

Make "date" times with your partner. This may sound simplistic but it is amazing how few couples block out time for each other in the weekly log. This doesn't mean necessarily that you'll leap into each other's arms and start making love the moment the clock strikes, but it does mean that you can enjoy the pleasure of anticipation knowing that a certain time of each day will belong to the two of you to use as you wish. You can choose to surprise each other with something special during these moments, or just enjoy the quiet, private time you have set aside. The time is rendered additionally precious by the fact that each of you made the effort required to carve this time out of a busy schedule.

Solving Time Conflicts

Most time problems in your relationship will arise when you disagree with your partner over how to use a particular segment of day, week, month, or year. Following are some steps and pointers to help you resolve such conflicts.

A. Become thoroughly aware of your difficulties and problem areas.

For example, does your partner understand how intensely you resent his watching TV every night after dinner until bedtime? Do *you* realize how you irritate

The Use of Time

him by conducting long-winded phone conversations with your friends and fellow club members?

B. Take responsibility for correcting those problems.

Rather than let your anger simmer inside, ask your husband to discuss his TV watching with you, and suggest changes. He may find his enjoyment of television enhanced by reducing the number of hours and selecting programs more carefully. For your telephone problem, consider that you probably will cover more ground in a given time by limiting your phone calls to five or ten minutes. Hour-long gossip fests may be tasty and titillating, but they hardly contribute to the health of your relationship with your partner.

C. Share your needs and problem areas concerning time with your partner.

Does it take you all week to clean house when the work should be completed in a day or two? Perhaps you don't know how to do a certain kind of work efficiently. Perhaps your partner can suggest ways to help you and free up time for more pleasant pursuits. Doing chores together serves the double purpose of cutting down the time spent on them while increasing time spent together.

D. Look for solutions which will incorporate your needs as well as your partner's.

Suppose your mate has a full-time job and you are a part-time real estate salesperson. He or she is at work five days a week (when you are home most of the time) but your job requires you to be with clients many evenings and weekends.

Both of you want more time together. But if he or she takes time off work to be with you, there is the risk of being fired. If you stay home in the evening instead of meeting clients, you will miss sales which are important to your family's economic health. What to do?

1. Either or both of you could change jobs, although this might cause more problems than it solves.
2. As a compromise (since both of you eat) you could arrange to meet for lunch or dinner several times a week. Besides allowing you more time together, this arrangement could add the romantic touch of your premarital dating, and you could develop a new mutual hobby of exploring restaurants. Also, the time either or both of you had spent previously in preparing meals at home could be devoted to discussions of your plans and activities.

E. Experience together and alone how these changes in your approach to time management change the quality of your daily life.

As you reduce your housecleaning and telephone time, you will become aware of time available for other pleasant occupations. And your husband can tell you how much he appreciates the fact that when he comes home he finds you relaxed and energetic rather than buzzing in a frenzy to make up for lost time in getting dinner.

F. Enjoy time. Make it work for you, not against you.

Time for Others

If time management problems revolved only around you and your partner and children, solutions would be relatively simple. However, both of you bring to your marriage your own families—mothers, fathers, brothers, sisters, aunts, and uncles—and you must arrange time for them in your life also. They are significant people to you, just as your partner's family, or specific family members, are

The Use of Time

significant to him. Yet accepting—and making time for—your partner's relatives is often difficult. Mother-in-law jokes are hackneyed for the very reason that mothers-in-law (and other in-laws) are a common source of conflict within a marriage. Your family associations, and time spent on this, cannot possibly have the same meaning to your partner that it does to you.

Suppose, for instance, that your grandmother—who is now old, dependent, and depressed—was the warmest, nurturing person in your life when you were growing up. Now in a nursing home, she depends upon you for comfort, attention, and small favors. Although she is crotchety now, you tolerate her moods out of the love she once lavished on you. But you cannot expect your partner to tolerate her in the same way, because he does not share your memories of her. You love her, but he is impatient with the time you spend caring for her. Then you become angry with him, because of what you consider to be an unfair attitude, and you have a dilemma.

It is important then to communicate with your partner and share the importance of your grandmother and other important family members in your life. If you can do this, your partner will see these people in a new light. As you deepen your understanding of each other's needs, you will be able to appreciate the other people in each other's life more deeply as well. These may be a special parent who helped build your confidence, a special sister who loved you when no one else in the family cared. Share these important people with your partner so that he can learn to love them for the same reasons you do.

Recall your childhood and relive your significant times with your family. In your workbook write their names, the events that remain vivid in your memory, what these people mean to you, and how you would like to relate to them now. Be specific. Recalling the pleasures of the "old days" will not only illuminate these people to your partner, but will also refresh your own loving memory of them. Here's an example:

Name	Memorable events	Feelings associated with them	How to relate now
Grandma Julie	Christmas, Summer vacation, Story-telling, Cared for my dog when he was hurt.	Love, Good food, Acceptance, Admiration.	Spend holidays with her, Send goodies and care packages to her nursing home, Spend hour each day with her.

Once you and your partner have each written in detail about your most meaningful close relatives, share your workbooks and discuss your entries. Almost immediately you will become more tolerant of his relatives, and he of yours. You will be sharing old memories and in effect bringing your partner closer to the loved relative.

Alice, for example, disliked her mother-in-law because the elder woman hovered over Alice's husband, Joe, like a mother hen—overprotective and solicitous about whether Alice was being a "good wife" to him. Alice dreaded her mother-in-law's visits because she knew she'd have to repress her own rage throughout the weekend. This was an ordeal which she dreaded although she tried to be kind to Joe's mother.

Finally—just before another visit—Alice exploded in anger and told Joe all her feelings about his mother. She was surprised when he agreed with her feelings and explained that he did not enjoy his mother's overprotectiveness either. Then he explained how his mother came to be that way.

First, Joe had suffered a great deal of poor health as a small child and his mother was abnormally fearful that he would die. Then, when he was three, two stepchildren by

The Use of Time

his father's previous marriage were brought into the home despite his mother's opposition. From that time, there was a division in the family. The father lavished his attention on his two older children, while Joe's mother felt that she must protect herself and her child against the intrusion.

"It was us against the world, you might say," Joe explained. "When I was little I couldn't understand why Mom disliked the other kids so much, but later all her fierce protectiveness made sense, even though she went overboard with it. Now, even though the old threat is gone, she's still the same way and I tolerate it."

Alice had never before heard the story of Joe's childhood, but from that time forward she was able to meet and relate to her mother-in-law with greater tolerance. The most important element in the change was her knowledge that Joe agreed with her viewpoint and sympathized with it. They approached the "lost weekends" of Mom's visits together rather than apart.

If you feel oppressed by the time consumed by visiting relatives, here are some steps to ease the problem:

1. Share with your partner the value of seeing and being with him or her alone. (Your partner may not know how keenly you feel about this.)
2. Try to relate to your partner's relatives as individuals, discover them as friends.
3. Don't lump all of them into a group such as "your relatives" or "my relatives." You might enjoy her sister's visit, but not her brother's. Or you might enjoy going on a picnic with his parents, but hate going to the theater with his gossipy cousins. Open yourself to the possibility of enjoying their uniqueness.
4. If it is too constraining for you to have people stay in your home for a period of time, reserve a place for them in a nearby hotel or motel. Politely ignore the

social pressure which says, "When your relatives come to visit us, we should . . ."

5. Another way is to change your "shoulds." Say to yourself, "When my relatives migrate out here next month, I will not spend every moment with them. We can send them off on side trips by themselves, and make it clear that we have our own family and social life to maintain. Leveling with relatives helps too."

6. If your spouse's relatives live nearby, he can visit them at *their* home while you do something else with your time. If he wants to meet his family's demands to see him regularly, it is not necessary for you to always be involved. Learn to say no tactfully.

The Outside World

We have discussed your management of time alone, with your partner, with your family, and with your relatives. However, the most voracious time tyrant is the outside world—the world of work, clubs, lodge meetings, and social involvement. Many marriages crumble gradually simply because one partner (or both) allows outside "obligations" to fill all his time, leaving virtually none for spouse and family.

Phil and Tina are a case in point. They have been married for ten years. Phil is a rising, young middle-management executive in a large corporation. Tina manages their comfortable home and is involved with a number of social and charitable women's clubs. They have no children because, as they say, "We'll delay that until we have time for them." Except that Phil and Tina have never found time for children.

During the early years of their marriage, Phil worked a normal nine to five job and hurried home for a pleasurable

The Use of Time

dinner and evening with his young, attractive wife. Later, however, he began staying late at the office to complete his work, or else bring work home with him to finish in his study after dinner. He advanced rapidly in his company and enjoyed his pay raises and the approval of his superiors. The more he received of both, the harder he worked.

As he gained recognition in his company, Phil also attracted the attention of community leaders in his city. He was invited to the local Rotary club and then a secret lodge which met one evening each week. He accepted committee assignments to raise funds for the Community Chest and YMCA. Soon most of Phil's evenings were filled with meetings away from home.

Thrown more and more upon her own resources (and needing some recognition in her own right), Tina joined a bridge club and branched out from that to holding office in several charitable organizations. The church guild also occupied much of her time. While Phil worked in his den or attended evening meetings, Tina lived on the telephone maintaining contact with club friends or organizing functions for her charitable enterprises. She saw her husband at breakfast, briefly at dinner, and again briefly as they retired for the night.

Several things, of course, were happening here as they happen in literally millions of modern marriages and relationships. First, Phil and Tina simply allowed the outside world to encroach upon and devour all of their time. Second (and this is common) Phil's ego satisfaction in his job gradually came to replace the quiet satisfaction of being alone with his wife. It was flattering to be invited to membership in important clubs and committees. It made Phil feel important. Third, as Phil's time was diverted from her and their home, Tina felt a great need for attention and consideration in her own right, and reached outward to friends, acquaintances, and clubs to fill the void in her life.

To their widening circle of friends, Phil and Tina

seemed to be the perfect couple with a nice home and all the material signs of comfort and happiness. However, now they began to suffer brief flare-ups of anger and resentment at breakfast and dinner because they no longer had time to communicate intimately with each other. They had traveled separate ways so long that each really did not know what the other was doing or wanted to accomplish.

Their marriage came to a crisis when Phil was approached by a group of community leaders who asked him to run as a candidate for city council. Phil was flattered and accepted the invitation. Tina held her temper until the delegation left, then she burst into tears.

"If you run for the council," she wailed, "I'll never see you again."

As usual in such cases, Phil had not realized how he had allowed outside interests to gradually fill all his waking time. More importantly, he had not been conscious of the fact that he had substituted the adulation of bosses and "important people" for his own wife's affection and warmth. There had simply been no time left for their marriage to grow.

Long into the night, Phil and Tina discussed the situation. She recognized she had been partly at fault by not leveling with him before the situation became critical but instead had found her own substitutions. They agreed that what they wanted most in the world was more intimate time with each other.

Next morning Phil called his friends and declined to run for the council. For both of them it was impossible to pull out abruptly from all their civic and charitable activities, but they gradually weeded these down to a minimum. And Phil discovered that he was considered even more valuable at work when he politely refused to take on extra assignments. He and Tina both learned to say "no" politely when they were called to provide volunteer time and labor.

The Use of Time

The world outside can devour all your precious time if you permit it. It is important that you learn to filter out "busy" work and time spent unnecessarily away from each other.

Learn to use your time alone and time together to enrich your relationship.

9
Managing Your Money

"Judy, will you come in here a minute?"

She was in the kitchen. Her husband, John, was in the study. It was the first of the month and he was paying the household bills.

"Okay," she thought with a sigh. "It's time for the monthly ritual." As she faced him in the study she resented the fact that he made her feel like a child about to be corrected.

"You've done it again," he said. "This month you spent 500 dollars more than I made."

"I bought something to wear to Madge's party," she said.

"I'm not questioning what you bought," he said, "but must you always patronize the most expensive shop in town?"

"I wear good clothes so that you'll be proud of me when we go out." She was trying not to be angry or argumentative. "You're widely known and respected, and I should think you would like my appearance to be in keeping with that."

"I don't object to your having a good wardrobe," John said with a sigh. "It's just that month after month we keep spending more than our income."

"Perhaps if I tried to get a job, it wouldn't be that way," Judy replied.

"We've gone over that, and you know why I feel the way I do about your working," John said, his temper rising. "The simple point is, my salary is sufficient to provide us a high standard of living and it's important for us to learn to live within limits."

"You're tellng me, then, that you're going to ration the amount of money I spend?" Judy said. "What you're saying is you're going to treat me like a child, that I will have no freedom of choice where money is concerned? Yet you won't let me work to have money of my own."

It was the same argument as last month, and the same stalemate. John and Judy both wonder how long their marriage will last if it goes on like this.

They *should* be concerned because, in our experience, money ranks along with sex and communication as one of the three greatest road blocks to happy marriage in American society. And money—the lack of it or misuse of it—can break up your marriage, if you allow it to. That's why it is so important to look closely at the meaning of money and its management.

Money symbolizes a number of different things to different people, such as:
- Power
- Possession and control
- Security
- Substitute for love
- Means to the good life
- Charity
- A nest egg

Let's examine each of these in greater detail.

Money as Power

One aspect of equating money with power is that we tend to idolize, respect, and envy those who have attained high positions and earn a lot of money. Unfortunately, most of us in America use money as the yardstick of success. We may know a person who is competent and yet does not have a high income. A conditioned tendency is to think, Okay, if he's so smart, how come he isn't wealthy?"

It is important to realize that not all people place such a high value on making money. Just because someone is not earning a grandiose income does not mean he is not a talented, capable person. It is erroneous to judge success merely in terms of money-making ability.

A second aspect of utilizing money as power is in the control of people and resources. A good example is the corporate president who owns the controlling interest in his business. His majority stock gives him the power to cast the deciding vote in any decision, which may involve the risk of capital in a new venture, or involve the welfare of his employees.

A third element in the possession of money is buying-power. Once a certain level of wealth is reached, you can purchase anything you wish from gourmet food to a luxury yacht.

Fourth, money is independence. Once you have it, no one else can tell you how or where to spend it. You may use it for any purpose you wish. That's certainly a form of power.

And, finally, money is often used to wield power over a mate (and this is what concerns us here). In cases where a wife (or husband) is totally dependent upon a partner's income, that partner may use money to control his mate's behavior and style of living.

It seems that the power of wealth often brings with it a measure of ruthlessness in dealing with other people. Once you have tasted this intoxicating power, there is a danger that you may use it against your spouse and family as well as others.

Money as Possession and Control

Traditionally, the man has been the main breadwinner in the family. However, since World War II, increasing numbers of women have entered the job marketplace at many levels. Today over forty percent of the work force is female. Women are buying themselves a measure of independence that is important to the "balance of power" between partners.

In those families where the man provides the sole support, however, he still has implicit control over his wife. He may not choose to exert it, but he has it. He may be generous with the purse strings, or he may choose to give her very little money to cover household expenses, and force her to beg for any extra money. Men thus can use money to possess and control their wives, just as many women use sex to manipulate their husbands. We hope society is moving away from both types of manipulation.

What happens when a husband plays with his power to give his wife a generous allowance or deny it to her? She begins to resent her enforced position of weakness and groveling. His attempts to control threaten her freedom to disagree and make independent decisions. He has created an atmosphere of fear, obedience, submissiveness—and resentment. Whenever these feelings predominate, there is an unavoidable crisis in the marriage.

What can be done to head off a crisis like this?

First, the wife can get a job and make some extra money. This is not always possible, of course, especially if small children need her care. But when it can be done, she will gain self-esteem from the feeling that she is sharing in the maintenance of a household, even if it isn't 50-50 sharing. She should at least feel that she has the right to get a job.

Even here, however, the working wife must move with caution. Some men may now be "liberated," along with their women, but many men still feel threatened by a wife who makes more money than they do. Most men probably still subscribe to the myth that they must be stronger, more intelligent, more competent in the working world than their partners. We hope this myth also is fading, but we still see couples that break apart over this issue.

Of course, the situation can be reversed. There are women who make more money than their husbands or mates do. However, women tend to be less manipulative when it comes to money because of their conditioning. They tend, in fact, to understate their high incomes and to spend time building their partner's ego if they are making more money. This goes a long way toward averting a crisis in the relationship. Still, there are times when a marriage suffers because the wife is earning more than her husband.

Although this type of relationship problem, in which the woman earns more money than the man, is still rather rare, it is obvious that such a situation should be discussed openly and candidly before it becomes a serious problem. It should not be a problem, of course. Marriage should be a joint venture in which each partner shares the other's work. If a man feels the need to control his wife through tightening the pursestrings, the relationship is on unstable ground to begin with.

Another more common version of the possession and control syndrome is the man who thinks his job is more important because he makes more money. If a child is sick or a chore demands attention away from work, the wife is the one who sacrifices because *his* job is more important. If you both work, and situations arise which necessitate one of you being away from work, learn to negotiate who should stay home. Try taking turns or splitting the day or days needed at home (he goes to work in the morning, she goes at night).

Again, all responsibilities should be shared equally. Because men have held the power in commerce and industry for so long, this will be slow to happen, but we do see it beginning to occur among younger people. Superior position or superior earning power should not be an excuse to use money as a possession and control mechanism.

Money as Security

Since withholding money may be used as a technique to control a spouse, it is not uncommon for two people in a relationship to maintain separate bank accounts. (It is hard to think of such people as "partners" because one wonders what level of trust holds the partnership together.) An especially sad version of this is the wife who squirrels away small sums of money from her household allowance and hides it so that she can buy some small measure of independence (such as a dress or expensive lunch) at some later date.

Many couples fight over the fact that the wife insists upon keeping her inheritance in a separate account, or the husband wants to maintain a separate account for his personal use and investment. This often happens in cases of second marriages, in which both partners had possessions and assets before entering into the new contract.

It is understandable that a person—particularly the

wife—might be fearful that her husband would squander her money as well as his own, but such fear is certainly a poor foundation for a close relationship. What such partners are saying, in effect, is, "I don't trust you with my assets, and I don't trust the marriage. The only thing I can depend on is my material security and I'm going to hold on to it."

In such marriages, the partners should level honestly with themselves and each other to determine whether or not the emotional security of their relationship is more valuable than financial security. Worrying about the loss of money does not make for a secure marriage.

Money as a Substitute for Love

When two people feel lonely and unloved, they hold on to anything that seems to give them substance. In such a relationship, each partner tries to punish the other.

She may buy expensive clothes or use charge cards excessively, thus buying more than they can afford to spend. She might suspect that he has been unfaithful and think, "If he doesn't care about me, why should I care about his pocketbook? He spends money in bars and taking friends out to expensive restaurants while I'm trying feverishly to prepare budget dinners on the nights when he does come home. No more!"

The husband, on the other hand, might reduce her allowance if the house is not neat, if she cooks unappetizing meals for him, if she hasn't been sexually responsive, or if she's not being as docile as he thinks she should be.

Both partners have the ability to use money destructively. What they may not realize is that money is the secondary issue. What they really want is more care, attention, and love from one another. Give careful thought to the possibility that this condition may exist in *your* marriage. If such symptoms are present, talk it out honestly with your partner. It is important that you reach agreement about the use and misuse of money and, more important, if you are using it as a substitute for love.

Money for the Good Life

Technically, money is a symbol, and an acceptable means for purchasing goods and services. Intrinsically, the value of the paper and ink on a $1000 bill is no more than a fraction of a cent. Thus, money is but a means to an end.

With sufficient money, you can afford a beautiful home, elegant clothes, exciting travel and vacations, expensive hobbies, and all the other goods and services that would appear to make you happy. However, experience has shown that many people with great wealth can be quite miserable and unhappy.

Happiness . . . joy . . . peace of mind cannot be measured in dollars. A poor child might be quite happy with a doll made from a stuffed stocking with shirt buttons for eyes and a mouth of stitched red thread; whereas a rich child might be unhappy with an expensive, imported doll complete with a full wardrobe of costumes. Thus, happiness or pleasure is not a function of the monetary value of an object, but rather of *how* one regards that object.

Partners may disagree as to how and when they wish to spend their available income, where to live or vacation, or how much to save and invest. This disagreement can result in discord and friction to the detriment of the rest of their relationship.

It follows—despite the amount of funds available or financial status of the persons involved—that they must plan and agree on their priorities. They must agree on how much to invest for current and future financial security, and compromise on how much and where to spend their money on essentials, and for goods and services for pure enjoyment or pleasure. Such mutual planning can enrich their relationship. A sound financial plan and program can eliminate a major point of present and potential friction.

We can conclude that without financial comfort, the problems of marital accord, communications, sexual compatibility, and emotional stability (peace of mind) become vastly more difficult. On the other hand, a realistic living budget contributes a great deal to removing impediments to inner contentment and harmonious relations with others. The important thing is for you both to communicate what you want and how you think your money should be spent.

Money and Charity

Do you give money to a charity, such as your church or synagogue, because you genuinely wish to help someone, or because it's a way to buy recognition for you in the community?

How much do you give?

Does your spouse agree with your answers to both of the previous questions?

It is good to have the money to give generously to others because your motivation for giving does not affect the end receiver. But charity can be a thorny problem in a marriage, especially if one partner is more intensely caught up in a "cause" than the other.

I can remember one woman—in this case a member of the Roman Catholic Church—who believed devoutly in helping missionaries in foreign lands. At the rate of one, then five, then ten dollars a week she "borrowed" from her household account to send money to the missions.

Her husband, a generous man himself, was puzzled when he gradually noticed that the dinner table seemed to contain less and lower quality food. He asked his wife about it, concerned that he wasn't providing enough money for this purpose. She confessed, uneasily, to what she had been doing.

"But why didn't you tell me?" he demanded.

"I was afraid you'd be mad," she answered.

"Well, I am," he said, "but mainly because I'm hungry."

Fortunately, his sense of humor saved what could have been a nasty and long-term disagreement in another marriage.

Obviously, there is no way to suggest to you how much or how little you should give to charity. The greatest gift is often when you have the least money to spare, but giving of your substance to someone who has less certainly can be a source of deep, inner satisfaction.

Just be sure you and your partner have full agreement and understanding in this area of handling money. If you don't agree, go back and negotiate.

Money as a Nest Egg

Inflation usually matches our growing hunger for material comforts of life so that it becomes increasingly difficult to tuck some money away for a rainy day. However, people need to build their savings. It provides a sense of security. But it would be surprising if you and your partner agreed totally on how much should be spent and how much saved.

One partner may believe in spending everything now, refusing to worry about the possibility of difficult times in the future. The other may wish to limit spending now, in order to have a luxurious vacation every year, or else harbor a genuine fear of poverty.

In this area there is a serious need for the two of

you to negotiate and reach a compromise. If unequal spending habits are already causing you problems, you might do well to write a mini-contract setting out the limits and provisions of what you want to accomplish. Remember, this is not a case in which one person is right and the other wrong. Rather, it is a difference of viewpoints. Each person is entitled to his or her view of how much money should be spent and how much allocated to savings. Also there should be a balance in investments—agreed upon in advance—among savings accounts, stocks, property, insurance, etc. Often the type of investment is more easily agreed upon than the question of how money slips away without any part of it going into savings.

One man, for example, liked to give his wife expensive presents—usually on no special occasion, but just for the pleasure of seeing her surprise and happiness. What he failed to realize was that she *resented* his gifts because their income was not high and *she* was trying to build savings for their future.

For a time she tried to pretend to enjoy the gifts because she knew they were an expression of his love (and incidentally gave a lift to his ego). The disparity of their viewpoints blew into the open one day when he drove up to the house in a new car and invited her to come for a ride.

In her words, "I really blew my stack. I raised so much hell that he took the car back and demanded return of his down payment. God, that was really awful. He was like a whipped puppy, but he never did it again."

Another couple, Edna and Marvin, had a different problem. For years, this couple saved to give their youngsters the best education that could be purchased. Two became medical doctors and the third an attorney.

Once the children were independent, Edna wanted to travel and spend more on their own pleasures. Marvin, however, had become so imbued with the saving habit that he wanted to continue saving for their retirement years. Edna felt they had sacrificed enough and wanted to live in the present; Marvin wanted to keep putting it off into the future.

They worked out a compromise which included some travel but also substantial contributions to savings. Edna did not receive as much pleasure as she wished, but was willing to give up some of it in the knowledge that her husband lived with the constant fear that they might be "wiped out" by some future catastrophe. She did not share his sense of insecurity, but respected his feelings just as he respected her need to "live a little" to make up for the years of scrimping and saving for the children's educations. They had a rich marriage in values far greater than money.

What Does Money Mean to You?

In the preceding pages, you have seen how some people use (and possibly abuse) money. Have you ever taken the time to determine honestly what money means to you? The following exercise is for that purpose. Write the statements on a page of your workbook and then rate yourself (honestly) on a scale of zero to three, as shown:

Don't think about	Don't do at all	Do moderately	Do often
0	1	2	3

1. Use money as a source of power.
2. Use money to control my spouse.
3. Save money to feel secure.
4. Substitute money for love.
5. Use money for the good life.
6. Give a lot of money to charity.
7. Give money to my children's education.

Now compare your responses with your partner's. Are you far apart in many areas? Can you see a pattern evolving? Once you see where your patterns differ you can more clearly see where to compromise.

As we have emphasized throughout the book, the process of negotiation and compromise is the way to solve most areas of conflict, including money arguments. Here is how one couple approached the problem.

Barry and Claudine had been married for ten years when they came to me for counseling. They had two incomes—Barry making $20,000 a year and Claudine earning $6,000 working part-time. They both wanted children, but had been putting it off because Barry did not believe they could afford it. In fact, they fought constantly because at the end of each month all their money was spent and they had no clear idea of where it had gone.

As a first step, I encouraged them to answer the seven-point exercise shown previously. I stressed the need for them to answer the points honestly, since their findings would become the cornerstone for their solution.

After they had gone over their answers together, we discussed them. It appeared that to some degree Barry considered money a source of power, but even more strongly he felt the need to save money for their future security. He had been born in a poor family and was afraid of poverty. Claudine, on the other hand, believed in using their money for the good life as it became available and, to some degree, she was using money as a substitute for love because Barry's job required him to be away from home a great deal. (This latter point, incidentally, came as a revelation to both of them. Barry assumed that hard work was a manifestation of his love and Claudine had not been fully aware that her shopping sprees were a substitution for his presence.)

Once these points were clarified, the two were directed to estimate how their money had been spent in the past year. After taxes, their disposable income totaled about $20,000. Of this, approximately $12,000 went for necessities—mortgage payments, utilities, transportation, and insurance—which left them about $8,000 for optional expenditures.

Without going into detail about how the $8,000 was spent last year, Barry and Claudine were asked how they wished to spend this amount in the *coming* year.

Claudine listed a month's vacation in Europe, $3,000; home remodeling and furniture, $2,500; new clothes, $1,000; and entertainment, $1,500.

Barry listed a new car (to replace one of two they owned), $150 per month after trade-in—$1,800; a two-week domestic vacation, $1,000; clothing, $1,000; power tools for his workshop, $1,500; sports equipment and country club dues, $1,500; and savings, $1,200.

With the figures laid out clearly before them, *and* without a need to make an immediate decision on any of the purchases, Barry and Claudine were able to see their priorities more clearly. Also, because both *wanted* to solve their problem, they worked together on individual items. Claudine asked why it was necessary to buy a new car since their two vehicles were only two years old. Barry suggested they didn't need an expensive European vacation.

Recognizing her husband's need to build a savings account, Claudine agreed to trade Europe for a domestic vacation. And Barry saw the wisdom of postponing the new car purchase for a year. Since she had compromised on vacation, he agreed with her entertainment budget. As they went through the remainder of the list, they came up with the following compromise:

Home remodeling and furniture	$2,000
New clothes (for both)	1,000
Domestic vacation	1,000
Entertainment	1,500
Power tools	500
Sports	500
Savings	1,500

At the end of their negotiation, Barry and Claudine wrote their agreement in the form of a mini-contract with each other. In that way, if either was tempted to go overboard on an item, the other could refer to the contract. They could then renegotiate, or stick to the original plan. They were also advised to renegotiate at the beginning of each year to account for changing income *and* changing needs and wishes.

As you negotiate *your* way into monetary compromises, there is one tool that will be most helpful.

Budgeting

It is important for you as a couple to decide how you want to spend your earnings. Add up how much you have available, after taxes, and then make an accurate list of the expenses you know you must meet. Subtract these from your total and you will know what you have left for optional spending and savings.

If you haven't done this before, it is an exercise you should do carefully the first time, and then do it for each month of the year throughout your life. Income and mandatory expenditures will change, just as you can expect some changes in the things you want from life.

Once a year, go over the figures in your income tax return. This will show you exactly how you spent your money and whether or not you stuck with your budget. This is a good time, also, to decide *between you* if you want to continue your past spending habits or make some changes.

In most families, one partner or the other becomes the bill-payer and bookkeeper. Whether or not you alternate this chore from one year to the next, it is important that *both of you know at all times how the money is spent.*

Buying on Credit

In the American culture, it is impossible to escape the barrage of advertising that urges us to surround ourselves with more and more material possessions. We can too easily be victimized by the peer pressure of keeping up with the Joneses, and through the medium of television, everyone else in the country becomes the Joneses.

Likewise, it is almost impossible to live without buying on credit. Certainly, few young people could afford adequate housing or transportation without the ability to borrow most of the initial purchase price. Credit buying, in fact, has become such an ingrained way of American living that it's almost impossible to borrow in an emergency if you haven't previously established a line of credit by borrowing and paying off an installment loan.

So the use of credit is of great value in our society. The misuse, or overextension, of credit is an insidious threat to financial welfare and a marriage-breaker of the highest order. Many people (and not just young ones) spend more than they can afford and pay for it later by going heavily into debt, borrowing more money at exorbitant interest rates, having major items repossessed, or, finally, declaring bankruptcy. All of these steps involve mental anguish that can be avoided if you will carefully consider your purchases, *together,* and buy only the things that will be of genuine value to you.

Above all, avoid becoming an impulsive buyer. This is like having a disease but, fortunately, it's a disease that can be cured. Because impulsive buying—by either a man or woman—usually indicates an attempt to compensate for other unfulfilled needs, such as love and affection. And compulsive buying of this sort only leads to tighter turns in a vicious circle.

Consider, for example, a young wife who buys hats

and purses because she feels her husband is not paying enough attention to her. Rather than supplying what she really needs, her husband gets another job, moonlighting for extra income to cover his wife's spending habits. Then his wife really bemoans her fate because he is never with her but is working all the time. Time after time we see couples struggling to achieve higher incomes to cover unnecessary expenditures.

Ask yourself, "What would I enjoy more, living in a $100,000 house and driving a $10,000 automobile while seeing very little of my spouse, or would we be happier with a house and car half that expensive with time leftover from work to enjoy each other?" The rich (or not so rich) widow is a common member of middle-aged society. Often their husbands are killed by the stress of making enough money to try to keep them happy.

Again, it is important not to make unilateral decisions about the making and use of money. This applies not only to spending habits but to investments as well. You, as a wife, may give your husband a free hand in investing your money after mandatory expenditures, but he may lose it without your ever knowing what investments he had chosen. This places unfair and unnecessary stress on him, even as it deprives you of your right, as an equal partner, to make investment decisions.

Both partners need to be fully aware of all money decisions, and often the mere process of reaching joint decisions and compromise can add to the joy of a marriage.

Money should provide you with the necessities of life, but it should also bring you joy. If it is a source of dissension between you and your partner, it is time to get together on this most important subject.

And please remember, the amount of money you have is never as important as the other riches each of you can bring to your partnership.

10
Children

To Have or to Have Not

As late as a generation ago, having a family was accepted as a natural consequence of marriage. And birth-control—for most people—was a haphazard conglomeration of half-understood devices or processes that sometimes worked and sometimes did not.

That situation has changed dramatically since the 1960s when the birth-control pill became available and the clouds of disapproval, which for so long had obscured frankness and truth in family planning education, were dispersed. This combination, coupled with more liberal laws relating to abortion and worldwide concern with the problems of overpopulation, has brought about a whole new way of thinking about the advisability of having children. Couples now realize there's a choice involved—not only when but whether or not. The U.S. birth rate has fallen to one of the lowest levels in history. Whereas a family of three or four children was once considered average, many couples now are opting for one, or two, or none. The motivations for this are wide and varied, ranging from the man and woman who simply do not care for the burden of children, to the couple that hesitates to bring new life into a world which seems to be plagued by crime, violence, and decadence.

Whether or not to have children is one of the most important, long-lasting decisions a couple can make. If you decide not to buy a house now, you can change your mind two or ten years from now. If you decide not to have a child now, it's difficult to change your mind much beyond the age of thirty-five. After that, it's too late to begin parenting. If you buy a car, and it turns out to be a lemon, you can keep it or unload it. The most you lose is money. However, if you have a child and decide later that you don't enjoy the loss of personal freedom—or that you're just not cut out to be a parent—what do you do then? Once you have a baby, it is (or should be) a commitment for life. And it will consume at least eighteen years of your prime time. That is a long time if you have made a poor decision.

What Does a Child Give You?

Why do some people decide to have children? Let's examine some common expectations.

If you are newly married and are evaluating whether or not you want to become parents, answer the following questions separately and then together. Using your workbook, elaborate upon your feelings and dreams about your child of the future. This exercise will help you to come to a clear (and mutual) decision about family planning. If you already have children, answer the questions honestly anyway. Whether your motivations for having them were self-

Children

centered or other-centered, your answers can tell you a lot about yourself and about your expectations for your children.

1. Do I want a child to prove my manhood or my ability to become a mother (thereby proving my femininity)?
2. Do I hope to experience through a child (vicariously) things that were denied to me as a child?
3. Am I trying to achieve, through a child, things I failed to achieve as a child?
4. Am I trying to save a shaky marriage by having a child?
5. Do I want a child as an outlet for affection while, at the same time, I deny that affection to my partner?
6. Am I conforming to traditional expectations that a couple should raise a family?
7. Am I trying to fulfill a maternal or paternal "instinct"?
8. Do I want children so that I can stay "young in spirit" and continue growing up with them?
9. Do I want children so that I will receive compliments from friends, relatives, and neighbors?
10. Do I hope to mold a youngster who will be the smartest, prettiest, best dressed, or the best athlete on the block—just as my parents tried to do with me, and failed?
11. Do I want children so that I will not feel a void in my life as I approach my later years?
12. Do I want children to "carry on the blood line," so that eventually I will know the pleasures of grandchildren?

As you can see, some of these reasons for having children are sound, while others are flimsy. Many people view having a child as a means to an end, rather than enjoying the child himself.

Two people should discuss the issue of children before they enter into a long-term commitment. However, in too many cases, the mates get lost in the passion of their love and do not give careful consideration to the most likely fruit of that love. The question should also be discussed repeatedly *after* marriage because couples, as individuals, often change their minds.

Following are more questions a woman should ask herself before deciding whether or not to have a family.

1. If I want children, then how many? (If more than one) how far apart do I want to space them?
2. Is a career more important to me than having a child?
3. Can I handle both successfully—a satisfying career with enough time and energy left to raise a family?
4. If I don't have a profession now, do I want to go to school for additional training? Do I want to have children after *that* period?
5. If I decide to have children in mid-career, will I halt my career until the children are ready to go to school? Or will this terminate my career permanently?
6. If I decide to go back to work soon after having children, will I have live-in help available at home, different baby sitters, or will I leave the children at a day-care center?

The man needs to ask himself some questions also.

1. If I want children, how many can I handle, both financially and emotionally?
2. Am I willing to participate in the daily care of the child?
3. Does my job require a lot of time away from home

Children

so that I would not be able to share in the responsibility of raising a child?
4. If my wife does not wish to go back to work after having a baby, will I be able to support the family on one income?
5. How do I feel about my wife going back to work and leaving my child to the care of other people?
6. How would I feel about my wife going back to school?

As you see, the man's questions are different from the woman's. He may have one set of reasons for wanting (or not wanting) children, while she may have others. In recent years, increasing numbers of men are choosing to help actively in caring for the children, but in most cases the man still keeps his work patterns and the main task of child-rearing remains with the woman. This means that most of the time the man does not have to be concerned about delaying or giving up his career.

When the two of you have compared your answers to the preceding questions, and discussed them, you should have a much better understanding of each other's position regarding children. Some feelings not covered by the questions may also surface. A man, for example, who remembers his mother's near-death in childbirth may oppose children because he doesn't want to subject his wife to this danger. A woman who was lost as a child among a large number of brothers and sisters may find the memory so distasteful that she wants no more than one or two children. A first-born woman who was forced to help care for younger brothers and sisters may abhor the thought of caring for more babies. Or she may find the prospect appealing since she is already experienced in infant and child-care.

There really seems to be no way that the work and pains and pleasures of child-bearing and rearing can be taught. Examine your attitudes toward children before you take the irrevocable step of having one. It is a large step to assume the responsibility for another person, so you need to force yourself to clarify your values, insofar as possible, in advance. Using your workbook, answer the following questions. Your answers should represent a distillation of what you have learned about yourself in the foregoing exercises and discussions with your spouse.

1. Why do I want children?
2. What are my expectations from them?
3. What are my goals for them?
4. How much am I willing to give of myself?
5. How willing am I to give up material comforts for them?
6. How much of my freedom am I willing to give up for them?

Obviously, this process is not as mechanical as computing statistics with an adding machine. Wanting and having children involves deep feelings for the simple reason that continuation of the species is instinctive. As a man or a woman, wanting a child may be as basic as the desire to see and hold the fruit of your love-making. Here are some good reasons for having children.

1. We enjoy children.
2. We are financially able to support children.
3. We have the patience to raise children.
4. We have the required time and energy to raise children.
5. We have enough love to give our children.

The difficult thing about this list is that you *can't know* all of these things *before* having a baby. You may not be financially able now, but hope to be later on. You may misjudge the level of your patience just as you may misjudge

Children

your time and energy. Of the five good reasons listed above, the most important by far is the last one. No matter how affluent or poor a family may be, if a child is loved by both parents, he or she is likely to grow up a good and loving person.

If both partners are well-suited for parenthood, raising a child can be a joyous experience. The moment of giving life to a baby is, for most women, the most creative and fulfilling time in life (especially through natural childbirth). Witnessing healthy growth, the brightness and talent of your child, seeing him achieve his goals, being friendly, loving, and loved by others are all gratifying experiences for both parents. It is not a happy experience, however, if one or both parents decide they should not have been parents after all.

Reasons for Not Having Children

We may feel wrong somehow, or guilty, if we do not want children but it is important to examine both sides of the question as honestly and dispassionately as possible. Here are some reasons for *not* having children.

1. We do not enjoy having children around.
2. We don't want our freedom stifled by caring for a sick child or searching for a baby sitter.
3. We are involved in our own professional pursuits.
4. We can't afford children and still provide for our own creature comforts and desires.
5. We don't want to live a life of self-sacrifice.
6. We don't have enough patience to raise children.
7. We don't want to make such a long-term investment (usually at least eighteen years).

You *should not* feel guilty if any or all of the above statements ring true for you. You don't have to want to bring children into the world. It's your life to live the best you can, the way you want to live it. The important thing is for you and your partner to understand each other clearly.

What If You Disagree?

Two partners are likely to disagree when it comes to the question of whether or not to have children. Their feelings for or against having children may be mild or strong. The husband may want only one child, while his wife wants a houseful to love. Or the man is anxious to have children, while the woman is concerned about continual interruptions to her career.

What do you do when one partner really wants a child —and is well-suited for parenthood—while the other partner is adamantly set against it? This presents a whole set of potential problems, but if the battle lines are that clearly drawn it is not a healthy decision to have children. Obviously, one partner would not be a good parent, and the child would suffer from the marital dissension to which it was an innocent contributor. Also, *whether or not* the couple went ahead to have children, one partner would always carry a burden of frustration and resentment because his or her wishes were not respected.

Let us suppose that a wife wants a child, but her husband does not. As an ultimate stalemate, he might withhold his physical love to be sure that she doesn't become pregnant. She could retaliate, of course, by taking a lover to father her child, but in either case the marriage is headed for destruction.

If the situation is reversed—the husband wanting a child but the wife refusing—a more subtle battleground is created. He could make love to her repeatedly, attempting to get her pregnant, but without his knowledge she could use birth-control techniques (or even have an abortion) to thwart him.

Here again, of course, the predictable outcome is that one or the other partner will stomp out of the marriage.

Because the question of whether or not to have children is so difficult to compromise, this decision should always be part of the premarital contract. Once you are married, you cannot reach a 50-50 balance that will make both partners happy. Obviously, you cannot be half pregnant.

Here are examples to illustrate the importance of reaching an agreement before marriage.

A man may come to a new marriage with children from an earlier relationship. His new wife wants children of her own and assumes, because he has already fathered children, that he would want more. He neglects to tell her that he wants no more children.

What happens after this wedding, of course, is that the new wife is not only stuck with the work of caring for children from his previous marriage, but is also denied the fulfillment of having her own baby.

The reverse of this is the woman who was first-born of six children and was required by her mother to help care for her brothers and sisters from the time they were infants. As a result, she has no desire to have children of her own. She goes to law school and meets a successful businessman. They fall in love and plan to be married. He tells her frankly of his desire to have a family, but because of her fear of losing him, she hides her feelings from him, hoping the situation will solve itself after marriage.

Obviously, equivocation is not a satisfactory answer. To repeat, the question of whether or not to have children (assuming of course that you are capable of doing so) must be answered between the two of you before marriage and be discussed periodically throughout your marriage until it is resolved. Sometimes you must make a very difficult decision.

Is it more important to me to be a part of this couple, or to be a parent—but perhaps a single one?

Although this is a difficult area for compromise, some reasons for not wanting children may be answered in other ways. If a woman, for example, fears the distress and discomfort of child-bearing, but her husband wants a family, they might adopt a child. If the husband is infertile, but they both desire a family, they may resort to artificial insemination.

If one, or both, does not want the work and loss of freedom involved in child care, they might go ahead and have a child with the mutual understanding that they will hire a full-time live-in nurse. This, of course, depends upon your economic condition and is a satisfactory arrangement only if both partners commit themselves to spending some quality time with their child on a regular basis.

Whether or not to have children is one issue which must be resolved. There are few options for compromise and at some point there is no "taking back" the decision.

The picture we have portrayed is a severe one, but actually most disagreements are mild and soluble. Often they have to do with numbers of children rather than having or not having any at all.

Child Care Roles

Once you have reached a mutual decision that you want a family, and that you're both well-suited for the task, there are more questions.

Who is going to do what after the baby is born?

Once upon a time this question would have been senseless. Obviously, the mother would stay home and nurture their little ones, at least until the youngsters were ready for school.

If your joint salaries justify it, you can hire someone to look after the baby while mother returns to work.

You may place your child in a day-care center while mother goes back to work.

An increasing number of men are now choosing to stay home part of the time and share in the work at feeding time, diaper changes, and laundry. Some professional partners, whose time schedules may be flexible, choose to work part time on alternate time schedules so that they have equal time for parenting and their careers.

Child care is beginning to become a more shared responsibility, which is a healthy change. In the past, men have been robbed of many joys of fatherhood by having a limited amount of time to spend with their children. And women, tied to the diaper pail, were robbed of many opportunities to realize their potential outside the home.

What about Jealousy?

Many men are troubled by the feeling that they do not share in parenthood. After the moment of conception they feel "left out," as the mother-to-be goes through the process of gestation and concentrates upon the new life to be born. As she grows larger and heavier with her burden, she becomes less and less accessible to her husband. As one man related:

"I was proud and happy when Rosy became pregnant, and for a while our love-making was even better than it had been before. She was somehow more sweet and tender and loving.

After a few months, though, she began to get big and

sort of withdrew into herself. I can't explain it very well but it was as though she and the baby were off in a world by themselves and it didn't include me. She'd let me feel when the baby kicked, but even that seemed like something that wasn't my proper business.

"We didn't make love at all the last month or so of her pregnancy. I guess we could have, but Rosy just didn't seem to need or want it. And even when we did, I felt as though I was intruding in the baby's world, even though I had helped to make him in the first place.

"It was a great feeling again when Charley was born. He was a fine, healthy kid, but I guess I wasn't prepared for the way a baby takes over a house—the whole thing. When I'd come home from work, it was bottles boiling on the stove, or formula being mixed, or diapers being changed, and he squalled a lot. Rosy was always exhausted, with her hair hanging down in strings.

"I thought it was too much for her and I tried to help when I was home in the evenings, or during the night feedings, but she wouldn't let me. She said it was her job and she insisted on doing it all. And when she wasn't doing chores for him she had Charley down on the floor on a blanket playing with him.

"My meals went to hell, which I overlooked for a while because I knew Rosy had to get used to the new routine, but also it seemed like she never had any time for me. It was always her and Charley and I was somewhere out in left field, bringing in the paycheck and keeping a warm house for these two.

"Maybe I'm exaggerating a little but, yes, I guess I was jealous. I didn't feel like Charley was mine at all. He was hers and I didn't belong to either of them. It'll change, I guess, when I get him out playing ball but it has been weird."

This man's complaint is not exceptional. Women *do* become enraptured with their child-to-be and, along with the added work, they continue to lavish all their care and attention upon their infants.

Whether you are expecting your first child or your fourth, let this be a rule: No matter how busy or preoccupied you may be, *make time for your husband;* and make time for both of you away from the children.

Continued Intimacy

No matter how rational you may have been in deciding to have a family, and how you would manage child care, it is not long before the child threatens to devour and demand every moment of your day and night. Therefore, if you are to retain the intimacy of your love for each other, you must deliberately plan and execute time together away from the children. It is all too easy (as the family grows) for your priority list to include nothing but children, so that when your partner needs you, you're too tired or there is no time to enjoy each other. Unless you remember that time is *your* property, you will lose control over it. If you let him consume all of your time, your child will become the most intimate enemy between you and your spouse. And if the mother is bearing the major burden of child care, in the traditional pattern, then it becomes father's duty and opportunity to do something about it. Some ideas are:

Arrange for a baby sitter and invite your wife out to dinner and the theater, at least once a week. She won't have time or energy to do this herself, and probably will resist because she feels guilty leaving her duties. But if you're forceful, the date can be fun and you will put back some romance in your life.

The surprise element can do wonders for your wife and again, by having it arranged with a reliable baby sitter, after the theater check into a motel and spend a loving night alone together. The quiet time alone will work wonders for a renewal of intimacy.

Time away from the children is essential. It is time for you to renew one-to-one relations, and it is also important that the children know that parents need to get away now and then for time with each other. It is a good idea for youngsters to be separated from their parents periodically, so everyone wins in this kind of arrangement.

This works, incidentally, whether you have one child or ten. Be aware that the intimacy of man and wife within the family system is threatened as the family grows. There are always more demands for time and care than you can provide.

- Children get sick.
- Children fight with each other.
- Children get angry and frustrated and throw temper tantrums.
- A child will be jealous of closeness between parents.
- One child thinks another is getting the lion's share of parental attention (sibling rivalry).
- A child needs help with homework.
- A child needs chauffeur service to school, friends' homes, music lessons, swimming pool.

And *that* list could be endless.

No matter how much they demand of you, you must protect yourself from being totally swallowed up by your children. Assert yourself and remember that your intimacy with your partner is nourishing. It is the key to a stable marriage. It is also a model to your children as a loving, close relationship between adults. Above all, let your partner know what you need! Don't let him flounder and guess while you play the martyr.

Children

What about Discipline?

Many marriages are strained by the disagreement of partners over discipline of the children. The stereotype of modern discipline is the child who does something wrong and the mother says, "Just you wait till your father comes home. He'll take care of you." This casts mother hypothetically in the "easy" role (because she didn't take direct control of the problem) and father becomes the frightful ogre who will inflict corporal punishment when he comes home. This is a good way to teach your child to fear and hate his father, and it is hellishly unpleasant for a father to feel that his only evening contact with son or daughter will be as a punishing avenger for wrongdoing.

In real life, of course, either partner can be the "softy" or the "meany." This condition reached fairly serious proportions in one family where a boy was born after most of the other children had already left home. In this case, the last born was like an only child, and his father identified closely with him.

Because the late child had been such a burden to his mother, she often seemed to dislike him. Also, as a strict disciplinarian, she tried to instill within him all the lessons she had learned during mistakes and successes with other children.

As a result, mother always said "no," and father always said "yes," to this boy's needs and wishes. If the boy was assigned a task, mother cracked down but father let him off easy. If the boy wanted a toy, father would give him the money but mother wanted him to work for it.

The parents were sensible and loving people. Both realized they were going too far in their particular directions. Dad knew he was too soft; mother gradually accepted the fact that she was too strict. They solved the problem (over a long period of time) by meeting every situation possible as a united front.

The united front is important because youngsters are master manipulators. (I don't know if they learn this from adults or whether they are born with it!) When they fail to get something from one parent, they'll play the game with the other.

Jane may say, "Mother, Dad says it's all right if I go to the birthday party if it's all right with you." Mother (not knowing if Jane has talked to her father or not) doesn't want to be the "heavy" so she says, "Well, if Dad says it's okay, I guess it's all right with me." Jane has manipulated her way to the goal, and though this case is a simple one, it may have been that *neither* parent really approved of her going to the party.

Some things you can do as a couple are:

1. Agree on the disbursement of money. How much do you give the children? Is it an allowance, or do they work for it at a certain rate per hour?
2. Agree on limits, whether it be time, money, or something else, so that you both stick consistently with the same message to your children.
3. If a youngster is apt to play both ends against the middle in getting permission for something, don't give him a definite answer until you have discussed it with each other as parents.

Whether you are lenient or strict, the more essential rule is that you present a united front to your children. A child may become confused about himself if one parent is relaxed and easy while the other is authoritarian, and that confusion can become more complicated as the child enters into adulthood.

Children

Roles and Responsibilities

As early as possible, each youngster should learn that he is a part of the family and, as such, has a role to play and duties to perform. Role assignments are important, although they change with age. Early on, every boy and girl should understand that mother is not the only one who does household chores.

From wastebasket-emptying to lawn-mowing, youngsters gradually grow in their ability to assume responsibilities, and this is what the growing-up process is about. They need to learn consistency of behavior and fulfill their assigned roles each day.

If they don't, how do you handle the problem. Do you ground them, shout at them, inflict verbal and physical punishment? Any or all of these may be appropriate or unavoidable at one time or another, but for consistency of behavior, it is better to communicate clearly to your youngster whenever you feel that agreements have been broken. Such communication contains six elements:

1. Consistency and unity concerning responsibility
2. Taking responsibility
3. Cooperation
4. Assertiveness
5. Family meetings, including "I" messages, listening, and feedback
6. Respecting agreements and contracts

Consistency

It is not enough to remind your child that he has reneged on an agreement, and then do the chore yourself. If you do that, the child comes to believe that there will always be someone to rescue him from his task. Always have your child fulfill commitments. Here, as in all aspects of parenting, parents should be consistent and united. Parent consistency teaches the child (through modeling) consistency in life. The message is, *If you start a job, finish it.*

Are you practicing such unity in relation to your children? Are you consistent most of the time? When do you fail to be consistent? Is it when you are tired, impatient, or unhappy about your marriage? If you feel uncertain in these areas, discuss them with your partner.

Responsibility

Responsibility builds self-esteem. Eventually, the child becomes proud of himself, proud of his ability to carry through his commitment in a responsible way. He learns to respect the closeness and unity of his parents and their value system.

Cooperation

Working well together requires positive energy, positive vibrations, and cooperation. The child needs to know that you are not operating under a double standard. Everyone in the family should do the chores assigned to him, fully and diligently. Youngsters are quick to pick up on a "Do as I say, not as I do" atmosphere. They will not work under such an arrangement, and neither would I. If Dad orders them to do their chores but he isn't doing his own, then that's inconsistent. That doesn't work when you are trying to create a cooperative environment.

If the family works together, a great deal can be accomplished in a short time. An example of cooperative teamwork may be garage cleaning day, probably on a Saturday morning. Before beginning, parents and children agree on a division of work tasks, and set a time limit for getting the job done. With everyone clear on his assignment—and in an upbeat mood—you can make a game out of the project.

Keep a radio on hand to provide music to work by, and take a pleasant break now and then with cold drinks or a cup of hot chocolate, depending on the weather.

Perhaps you would like to set up a reward at the end, such as a pizza dinner. At that time, when the job is done, you can savor the feelings of closeness, fun, play, and accomplishment that you enjoyed together.

Has your family experienced such times of pleasant cooperative effort? Does it happen seldom or often? If it is seldom, discuss the problem with each other. What is missing? How can you improve your relations? How can you improve your working habits? It may be surprising how much input your children can provide in answering these questions and, by so doing, they contribute directly to family closeness.

Remember, blame and accusations are not constructive when you are trying to make positive changes. Each family member can make a small change to improve overall teamwork. If one family member improves, compliment him or her and others will follow.

Assertiveness

Learn to assert yourself positively, but without anger or arrogance, to your children and your partner. Be sure they understand clearly what you want and need. Although the other person may deny your request, understand for yourself and help your children to understand that rejecting a request does not mean rejection as a person.

Do not "pull rank" as an adult unless it becomes absolutely necessary. Explain why you say "no." It is not enough to veto a request because you are a man and the boss of the family. Also it is not enough to do this because you are a woman and therefore allowed to be moody or bossy. After you have explained a refusal, the other person may still disagree or feel unhappy, but at least he will have a better understanding of your feelings and reasons for your position.

Family Meetings

A family meeting is a specially assigned time when each family member can express his needs and feelings openly and honestly. This promotes an atmosphere of open communication.

If you have not been in the habit of holding family meetings, the first one may be strained because the children may be suspicious that this is another occasion for the parents to deliver a lecture. However, once they learn that this is an open forum—that each person, no matter what age, may say what he likes or dislikes—the meeting can be productive and even fun.

One family, for example, makes a festive occasion of the event. Parents and children take turns arranging the meetings, which are held on Sunday nights. Whoever is in charge sets up a small discussion agenda and also determines what refreshments will be served and what games the family will play after the more serious part of the meeting is over.

Here, again, negotiation and compromise are essential to a good family meeting. Susan at sixteen, for example, may state that she feels it is unfair that her parents require her to be home at 10 o'clock every evening, even if she's at a party or on a date.

Father asks, "What do you think would be fair?"

"Well, I'm growing up," Susan answers. "I think I ought to be able to stay out until midnight."

"Every night?" Father asks.

"Oh no, I don't mean that. I just mean on party nights when all the other kids are out."

"I think Susan is growing up, too," Mother comments. "I believe we can trust her, and as long as she gets enough rest and keeps up with her homework, I think she might stay out until midnight on special nights." (Turns to the rest of the family.)

"Do you think it would be fair if Susan stayed out till midnight on Friday or Saturday nights if she has a special party or date?" (Heads nod, even smallest child has a vote.)

"Could you live with that, Susan?" Father asks.

"Yes, I could," she answers, and chances are, having been a party to the negotiation, she will keep her commitment.

During the family meeting—as elsewhere—keep in mind that being assertive does not mean being stubborn and unreasonable. Assertiveness is being yourself, knowing your self-worth, and being fair and reasonable. Express your wants and ask to be heard, but also learn to accept the reasoning of others if it doesn't happen to match yours.

In family meetings, the children may force you to re-examine your relations as partners. They serve as mirrors. You cannot teach assertive behavior if you yourself are not comfortable in being assertive.

Do you assert yourself with your children and your partner?

Are you encouraging them to be assertive without being unreasonable?

How can you improve your assertiveness without alienating your children?

Answer these questions for yourself, and then discuss them with your partner and your family.

Agreements, Commitment, and Contracts

Children need to know the value of a commitment. Out of the many mini-contracts kept in various daily life situations, one learns to respect and honor the bigger contracts of life. Keeping promises and agreements in the family is of highest importance. You may use written agreements if the process seems comfortable to you. Writing seems more binding than verbal promises and there is less room for misinterpretation later on. For example, if a boy fails to keep his promise to empty the wastebaskets every day, you can show him in writing where he promised to do so.

As an experiment, plan the weekly responsibilities and assign duties to each family member. Also include how you, as a family, are going to spend time together during the week. Once all this is written down, then each member of the family signs it.

Learn to honor your signature and the written mini-contract. If one or more members of the family fail to fulfill their commitments, call a family meeting and ask the person or persons who did not fulfill their obligations to express his feelings about why his promise was not kept. Others may comment as well but they should not express themselves in a blaming way so that one "black sheep" feels like a criminal. Review assignments and note where outside commitments (such as homework, football practice, glee club, or even Dad's and Mom's work) may be interfering with family duties. It may be necessary to reassign jobs, and where children see that this is done fairly, it will build their respect for their contracts as well as others.

Children

Pain and Disappointment

How do you deal with pain as a parent? Children, after all, seldom follow the exemplary pathways we envision for them. Can you be honest with yourself and your partner and express your worries? Can you share the suffering you sometimes feel about your children? Pain (when a child has done something wrong) often is associated with the idea that you've "failed" as a parent.

We view children as extensions of ourselves. If reality does not dovetail with what you had in mind, you are disappointed. Can you level with your child and share what you're feeling without burdening him with guilt and obligation? This is one of the most difficult problems in rearing a child to adulthood.

How do you cope with a sick child? Short-term illnesses we can anticipate and handle. But what about a child who is chronically ill or handicapped? Are both parents sharing in the care? Do you recognize the breaking point at which it becomes necessary to hire special help or place the child in an institution?

If this child demands more than you can give, physically or mentally, can you be honest with yourself and your partner and do less, or share the load? Can you (as sometimes becomes necessary) make your child understand that the burden is too great so that he will demand less of you? Can you do this without ruining the child's self-esteem?

Parental Rescue

Many times we cannot bear to see our children in pain and go to their rescue. We try to protect our boy or girl from difficult situations; we resolve their problems by doing homework, mediating quarrels with friends, and settling disagreements with teachers. The rescuer in us means well, but it does not serve a good purpose.

By not allowing a child to solve his own problems, we create dependency. We also create resentment, although it may not be immediately apparent, by depriving him of the opportunity to meet challenges and grow, to be a winner after struggle and defeat. Frustration and failure are a part of any life, and each of us must grow through the experience of pain and defeat. By sheltering your child, you delay his confrontation with real life.

Letting Go

As the children grow up, you face new joys and new problems. They need you less and yet there are new needs. The teens are trying and difficult, but your child needs freedom to test his independence. He should be ready to make decisions about school, friends, how to spend his leisure time, and how to relate to you at home.

As a common example, your child may leave his or her room untidy for days at a time. You must make a choice as to whether you will allow him to discover his own standards of neatness, or if you will force your standards upon him. One rule that works in many homes is that in common areas everyone is responsible for picking up after himself. In their own area, they may leave it as untidy as they wish for as long as they wish. (It is important, however, that you and your partner agree on the form and style of discipline and maintain an atmosphere of consistency.)

In regard to safety rules and moral conduct, if you have taught them well as small children, they should not require that you nag them persistently on these subjects later on. Unfortunately, many children must learn life's hard lessons by being hurt. There is a fine line between caring and overprotectiveness, and you will have to find yours for yourself.

Letting go—resolving your needs to protect and possess your children—is a growth process for the entire family. Our children's independence and their ability to take responsibility for their lives, their mistakes, and their accomplishments, are your rewards for effective parenting.

Then You Are Two Again

Finally, your children leave home—to college, to jobs, to marriage, and to new homes of their own. True, the fledglings are likely to return to the roost for shelter now and then, but sooner or later—if you and your partner live so long—you will be alone together once more.

The nest is empty. Psychologists, in fact, expect to find the empty nest syndrome, especially among women who had devoted full time and energy to caring for their families and now find little to keep them busy or interested. The house—not long ago a loud, brawling, untidy mess—now is too neat and too quiet. Now you tend to forget the unpleasant episodes, the bone weariness of trying to keep up with a house full of kids, and remember the good times and joy they brought into your life. However, it is not wise to let your life get stuck with nothing but memories.

Now is the time for new directions and rediscovering the intimacy that welded you to your partner in the beginning of your relationship. If Mother didn't work, she can think about a career, or she can find new hobbies, or go back to school. Father can use the money, once diverted to children, for investments and building a bank account for the future. Or he may be able to reduce his working hours so that he and his partner can spend more time together in recreation and travel.

The danger to guard against here is that many couples

have devoted so much time and energy to their children that they no longer find each other interesting or attractive. A common symptom of the middle-age crisis for both men and women is that when the children, the primary motivation for their effort together, are gone, many marriages break up. The divorce rate among middle-age couples is growing at an alarming rate.

Knowing this danger permits you to plan for the future. Think about what you will do when the children are gone, and find some good reasons to spend your later years together. Think of these advantages when the kids are gone:

- You don't have to get up in the morning to fix breakfast and lunch bags for school.
- You are not confronted by children's insatiable demands for money.
- You can read or visit art museums or have lunch with friends.
- You can find new ways to play and enjoy yourself.
- You can indulge in a hobby you've been setting aside for years.
- You don't have to cook big meals for hungry teenagers.
- You will not disagree with your spouse about child discipline.
- You don't have to lock bedroom doors. You can enjoy intimacy with your spouse at any time, anywhere in the house.

When your last child enters high school is not too early to begin planning how you and your partner will change your lifestyle when the children are gone. You can now do things which were prohibited while the children were still home and dependent upon you for food, shelter, and transportation. You can plan to move to a new smaller home, or plan some golden years traveling and relaxing.

The empty nest may well be the trigger which sets you on the path to creative retirement. Now you have more time for physical fitness. You have time to relax and cultivate new friendships. You may discover and develop new talents such as painting, writing, or woodworking. You may learn to play a musical instrument.

The fact is, your freedom of choice when the children leave home and at the time of retirement is almost as broad as when you were selecting careers as young men and women. It is never too late to do things you really want to do. The trick is to define them, and then to have fun getting there.

Relating to Grown Children

There is another pleasant aspect to your later years as a couple. Your children may become friends with you and among themselves. By now you can relieve yourself of the duty to change and control their lives and, oddly enough, once children leave home the more likely they are to listen to your ideas and advice. Here are some things you may do with your grown children:
- Discuss their higher education.
- Discuss their career plans.
- Talk about the pros and cons of marriage.
- Discuss investments.
- Become friends rather than parents.
- Give support without imposing your beliefs or opinions.
- Accept their values without trying to change them.
- Enjoy (but don't demand) their visits.
- Accept what they give freely, but don't expect more than they are willing to give of time and attention.
- Play with them.
- Share your life experience.

This new relationship with your children can be most

enjoyable, but only if you stop clinging to them for your own emotional satisfaction. Give advice if it is asked, but don't be disappointed if it is not followed. And *do not* try to select your child's mate or intimate partner. Your son or daughter may choose to live with someone quite alien to you, but remember—it is their choice and the life is theirs to live. You may not like a son- or daughter-in-law, but you may be surprised at how acquaintanceship can turn into love later on if you permit it to happen.

Finally, Grandchildren

The myths of grandparenthood are almost as pervasive as myths about marriage. Of course, grandparents spoil their grandchildren. You can play with them and even enjoy their childish boisterousness, because you know they'll soon go home and their upbringing is not *your* responsibility.

One cardinal rule is do *not* try to impose your values and morals upon your grown children as they begin the struggle with children that you began a generation ago.

And now, a new checklist. Answer the questions in your workbook:

1. How do I feel being alone again with my partner?
2. How do I feel about our years ahead, together?
3. What kind of relations do we have with each of our children?
4. Do I accept every one of them as a separate and grown-up individual?
5. What do I wish to improve in our relationship with our children?
6. How can I help you, my partner, to find new reasons to feel significant—and happy?

11
Managing Friendships

Most people need friends, and some need more than others. This statement seems to be almost embarrassingly simplistic, and yet friends—whether of the same or opposite sex—can be a tremendous source of irritation and dissension, as well as strength, in a marriage.

It is acceptable in our culture for women to confide in other women, to commiserate, to share feelings and secrets with one another. Men in our culture supposedly do not need and thus do not share their feelings with other men. This is a misconception, of course, because men *do* need and have friends—some at work, some for golf, some in clubs, and some for drinking and card playing. The fact that men are reluctant to discuss personal problems intimately with friends does not indicate a shallowness of feelings toward friends. Rather, it is a result of the fact that men have been taught to keep their feelings to themselves while women have been more encouraged to share their feelings with friends.

The word *friend* is one of those imprecise words that

convey different meanings to different people. Some people use the word to describe only someone dear to them—someone in their primary circle. Others use the word casually. A friend to them may be someone just to share a movie and a bag of popcorn. (We prefer the word *acquaintance* for someone with whom we have a superficial relationship and *friend* to denote someone with whom we enjoy intimate sharing.) The difference between a person who has many friends and one who has only a few may well be no more than the difference in definition. Most of us can count the intimate friends of a lifetime on one hand.

Because friends may either interfere with or enrich a marriage, we need to ask ourselves, "Do we need friends? What do we need them for? Do we both have the same values where friendship is concerned? What is your definition of a friend?" Think about it and try writing some thoughts on this subject in your workbook. This is a beneficial exercise because it may illuminate some aspects of your relationship with your partner, such as expressions of jealousy.

Here are some sample descriptions of a friend:
- A friend supports me and is uncritical.
- A friend is reliable and trustworthy.
- A friend may chide me in a loving way so that I can relate to the criticism and learn from it.
- A friend is someone who accepts me as I am—for *who* I am rather than *what* I am.
- A friend is a person with whom I can feel close physically.
- A true friend will accept my imperfections.
- A friend will tolerate and accept my silence.
- A friend is someone with whom I can share my most intimate thoughts.
- A friend is someone to trust.
- A friend is someone you can get angry with (without fear of losing him or her).

- A friend is someone you feel *safe* with—emotionally and physically.

Your Partner as Your Friend

Your partner is, or should be, your friend—in fact, your *best* friend. This is an aspect of a relationship that transcends and augments love. You probably spend more time with your spouse than with any other person, and he or she sees more sides of you than anyone else. And yet there can be cases when your partner is not a good friend. As one woman complained, "He is not my friend. I can't open up to him because he always judges me. I am afraid to express my feelings because he is angry when I am sad or when I disagree with him."

What she is saying is that she cannot accept her partner as a caring friend unless he can listen without being judgmental, unless he can accept her the way she is—sometimes sad and disagreeable as well as sometimes happy and agreeable. At first her husband was offended by her comment.

"How can you say I'm not your friend?" he demanded. "I'm your husband! I support you and live with you."

Later on, when her husband realized that he *was* in the habit of putting her down, that he *did* judge her behavior, interests, and opinions, he decided to change his ways of reacting to her. He *wanted* to be her friend. They also agreed that whenever she was sharing something with him, and felt he was judging her, she would tell him immediately how his comments sounded to her. She would make it clear, *at that time,* that she would not continue with her sharing when she perceived his feedback to be judgmental.

Thus, partners who are not friends can become so, but even when you *are* each other's best friends, it is not realistic to expect that all your human needs can be met by one individual. We therefore seek and cultivate additional friendships. Friends fulfill various needs for people and it may be well to dwell on some of these in greater detail.

Friends can provide *support* and a feeling of *security* —knowledge that someone is there in case you need help.

Friends may *substitute for family* if relatives are far away. You might create a circle of friends with whom you spend holidays, birthdays, vacations.

You may choose friends for *specific activities*—to dance with, to hike with, to play tennis with, to exchange child care.

You may choose friends with whom you *share a common bond*—people you work with, are attending school with, or who live in your neighborhood.

You may have *special talents or interests* which your partner does not share. Instead of depriving yourself, you can find other people with whom to share these interests, such as hobbies, museums, music, donating time to charitable causes, etc.

In forming friendships for all these various reasons, there is a common strand of belonging, caring, and of being cared for by others. It is important to our self-esteem that we experience those feelings.

Assessing Your Personal Friendship Needs

Before we can deal with the effect of friendship on your marriage, we need to examine some of the functions friends fulfill for the two individuals in the relationship, and we for them. Define the qualities *you* look for in friends. On a page of your workbook, divide the list into categories as in the following example.

Managing Friendships

Personal needs	Intellectual needs	Social and entertainment needs
good listener	intelligent	good sense of humor
empathetic	articulate	enjoys movies and concerts
not judgmental	curious	likes dancing
growth and change oriented	open-minded	likes good food and drink
honest with themselves and with me		
physically demonstrative and warm		

Now write the names of your friends under the appropriate category according to the needs they fulfill for *you*. You may find that some fit more than one category, indicating that they are compatible with you in a broader range of areas.

In going over this six months or a year from now, you may drop some names from the list or add new ones in one or all categories. One thing this exercise will demonstrate to you is the common fact that most acquaintances and friendships are transitory. Some friends remain with us for a few months or a few years, but only a rare few can be counted on for life, and often we find ourselves far removed from the ones who mean most to us.

One reason for the transitory nature of friendships, of course, is the increased mobility of our culture. Our parents may have lived all their lives in one neighborhood and close to the same people, but how many of us now live in the area where we were born? Because of all these changes, people now contact many new people all the time. We therefore have more opportunities to develop new friends, while often losing touch with old ones.

In addition to mobility, our culture is also changing in other ways at an accelerating pace, and we tend to change with it. As we change, so do the people with whom we wish to share time, ideas, and interests. If we seek lifetime friends, we are likely to be disappointed, except for the rare cases already noted. It is more realistic to consider friends to fill our current needs, and friendships to last only so long as it is comfortable and pleasurable for both of us. Some people find it hard to adjust to the transiency of friendships, while others adapt to it more easily. Basically, we need to learn to accept people for what they are, and what we can give to each other, without expecting more than either is able to give.

What Is a True Friend?

Like a rare wine, it requires most of a lifetime to distill a very few fast and true friends. But how do you identify one?

This is really quite simple. The true friend is the one who will answer your call for help if you need him or her, and to whom you will respond in turn. He or she is the person you don't hesitate to call—even if you're separated by a thousand miles—when you need a listener, when you want to share a tragedy or a joy. There are many ways in which a friend can express closeness and caring but the main one is to be *available*.

Friendships grow by giving. They also grow by receiving. Can you accept gracefully when a friend wishes to give to you?

Following is an exercise to assess your "true" friends. Write their names on a sheet of paper in your workbook, and test them against the following questions.

1. Can I call them (or him or her) without advance notice and invite myself to a visit at their house?

Managing Friendships

2. Can I call them without advance notice and ask them to spend an hour or a day talking with me if I need help?
3. Would this friend drop what he or she is doing to help me in an emergency?
4. Would I drop what *I'm* doing to help him or her in an emergency?
5. Would this friend listen to my personal problems and sympathize without passing judgment?

Take this exercise a step farther and answer the following questions in your notebook.

1. How many of my friends extended themselves and did something special for me during the past year?
2. In what ways did they help me?

At first thought, you may say "nobody" or perhaps only one friend provided something you needed. Or perhaps no one did anything for you because you *did not ask*. Most people are embarrassed to reveal a weakness or ask for a favor, but *how can they know if you don't ask?* Asking for what you need is as important in friendship as in all the areas of marriage we've covered. Your *true* friends would be hurt if they knew you had a problem but did not call on them for help.

If you have trouble asking things of friends, practice asking little things, such as, "I've got a problem that's bothering me. Could I come over and talk to you for a while?" or "I'm having trouble making a decision about buying a new refrigerator. Could you come with me and give me your opinion?" or "I'm going to go nuts if I don't get away for a weekend. Could you take care of the kids for me?"

The opposite side of learning to ask, of course, is

learning to give. You may discover that you ask for more than you give, that your friends are not asking you for help. Sometimes you need to go out of your way to offer your ear, your concern, your sympathy. How many times during the past six months did you actually do something for a friend, or let him know you were available if he needed you? One person calls her friends periodically and says, "I know we haven't seen much of you for a long time, but I just want you to know that if you need us for anything, we'll be there."

It is important, of course, not only to make the offer but to be sure you're prepared to follow through. *That's* the mark of true friendship.

Friends and Marriage

Although we should all recognize that no one person can satisfy all of our needs for conversation, attention, and companionship, we still find many couples who feel that their love should be all-encompassing and exclusive of others. When one partner feels this way but the other does not, the result can be unreasoning resentment and jealousy. The fact is that every person comes to an intimate relationship with his or her own circle of friends and also makes individual friends after the marriage. Learning to deal with those relationships is an integral part of making a marriage work. A young husband, for example, may deeply resent the fact that his wife has friends on the job who share her fascination with her profession. Or a young wife may resent her husband's need to play golf with friends. It is unreasonable to expect that your partner will automatically accept your friends as his own.

Harry and Lois, for example, met on a university campus and began dating. Her home was in the college town, but Harry's hometown was several hundred miles away. As they became more intimate, Lois thought she was doing Harry a favor by introducing him to her friends and inviting him with her to their parties.

Her friends accepted him congenially but Harry felt like a stranger, excluded from their private circle and often embarrassed when he could not share their private jokes. At parties, Harry was often forced to share Lois with other young men whom he assumed had courted her before.

During their courtship, he was especially resentful of Lois's best girlfriend, who had recently married. Occasionally, when he called her for a date, he found she was staying overnight at the girlfriend's house. Also, the other girl's husband, an old friend of Lois, had special jokes that he shared with her. Harry had an imaginative and jealous nature, and imagined that the other girl's husband made sexual advances to Lois, even though her relationship with the couple was strictly platonic.

Before they were married, Harry and Lois had their most serious quarrel over these friends. At first she was angry with his resentment and jealousy, but then Lois realized that Harry was more valuable to her than her friends. So she saw less of them, although she missed the carefree times she had enjoyed with the "old gang." After they were married, Harry was able to place his jealousy in perspective and learned to like certain individuals among Lois's friends, although he never felt close to them.

This is not an unusual example, but the fact remains that friendships outside marriage are essential to everyone. As a relationship grows and matures it is also logical that each partner—and the couple—will make new friends. Then the problem becomes one of managing friendships so that they do not cause a breach in your marriage. This is not to suggest that friendships are negative. Quite the opposite is true. Outside friends can enrich your life as an individual and as part of an intimate partnership, but if you spend too much or the wrong time with them, you're asking for marital difficulties.

What can you do when your partner spends more time with his friends than you feel is necessary?

For one thing, if they are not busy during the day he can meet them then. That can be considered his private time to use as he wishes, but he should arrange it so that it does not infringe upon prime time with you. If you and your friends are busy during the day, you can set aside one evening per week to be with them. Your partner can use that time to meet with *his* friends or use that time however he wishes. It is important, however, that both of you know (and agree upon) how this time is being used.

If your partner does not like this arrangement, check out why. Do not allow resentment and frustration to accumlate. Is he lonely? Is he jealous? Does he mistrust you? Does he feel that he possesses you, that he owns your free time?

If time to relate privately with your close friends is essential to you, then your partner must accept this. Jealousy is often irrational and unjustified. It can stem from insecurity or from a sense that one possesses his partner. Yet, if you feel jealous, you *own* the jealousy. It is a valid and legitimate emotion to *you*. If you are jealous of the time your partner spends with friends, you must express honestly how you feel about a specific friend rather than generalizing that he is leaving you alone and spending too much time with others.

As we have seen, time is amorphous, difficult to account for unless you make a specific effort to measure your use of it. As an exercise, keep a daily log in your workbook for two weeks of how much pleasant, quality time you spend with your spouse. (Do not count sleeping, gardening, or work.) Also note how much time you spend separately with friends. By reviewing this log, you may be able to determine if your spouse is justified in claiming that you spend too much time with friends. Of course, "too much time" is also hard to define. In a closed marriage, your partner may consider one night a week away from him too much. A person in a freer, trusting, and committed relationship may consider four nights a week to be excessive. It differs from person to person and from relationship to relationship.

Negotiate a compromise. Don't use your feelings to block your partner's freedom. Your hurt feelings and your insecurity can be manipulative and might create resentment.

For example, if your husband has been out three nights this week with "the boys," it is not enough for you to beg or demand that he give up that pleasure to be with you. His automatic reaction will be resentment that you're trying to control him. Rather, try to find a time when you're both in a good mood to negotiate your compromise. Then use "I" statements so that he will know how you feel, such as, "I was lonely and frightened when you were gone the past two nights. I want you to enjoy your friends but I can't help feeling jealous when they take you away from me." Out of this approach, you may reach agreement that he will limit his time with friends to specific times, or you may volunteer to entertain *them* at your home for an occasional poker party. Another approach is to agree with him (or her) that when he is out with others, you will use that time also to be with your outside friends.

Ask yourself the following questions.

What can I do for myself to feel secure when my partner needs time to be with his friends? Possible answers might be: Call Ethel and go to a movie; Visit mother and the family; Catch up on my hobby (such as painting or music); Call club members for volunteer community work; or, Help in a hospital or convalescent home.

How can my relationships with others become more meaningful? You might call an acquaintance for lunch or another activity to get to know him or her better; or offer solace or help to a friend of your own.

How can I accept my partner as an equal and free individual? This is difficult for most people—to realize that even though you have a close relationship, your partner is still a free individual. If you try to possess, or hold too fast, you may lose him or her.

What are my compromises to his or her needs—ones that I can live with and still feel good?

Be sure to set aside some time each day to spend quality time with your partner. Look for ways to become closer friends *with each other*.

What is the difference between the friendship with your partner and the friendships each of you may have outside your marriage? Is the quality of outside friendships better than the friendship with your partner? Is there something you can learn from this that you might incorporate into your marriage friendship?

Friendship Boundaries

If you need friends, you need to allow time to cultivate them. You must set your own schedule of how often to meet them, taking into account their needs as well. If it is enough for you to meet with a friend four times a year (yet she feels she would like to see you once a month), try to find a compromise between your two wishes. If a friend uses your valuable time in idle chatter and gossip, find a way to limit his or her visits. Remember that the time you choose to spend with others, and how you spend that time, are *your* decisions.

Friendship as a Couple

After analyzing what friendships mean to you and your partner as individuals, you are ready to plan your social activities as a couple. Following are some questions to settle between you. Discuss them and arrive at compromises you can both live with.

1. *How often do you wish to entertain at home?*

This is the most intimate form of getting together. It is private. You are sharing food with friends. Agree *together* how often and with which friends you wish to share this level of intimacy.

2. *How often do you want to go out with friends?*

Some people find this arrangement easier. They meet friends at the theater, for example, and perhaps end the evening discussing the performance over coffee and cake. The advantage of this arrangement is that you don't have to spend time cooking and preparing for them. The disadvantage is that it is less private and personal than meeting in your or their home.

3. *What kinds of entertainment do you like?*

a. Dinner Parties: It may be that your husband likes to bring business acquaintances and their wives to your home for dinner, but you are frightened and embarrassed that your cooking or manners of serving may not be adequate for such guests. You should clearly understand each other's positions.

If you hold dinner parties, you and your partner definitely should work as a team. He might serve drinks while you complete the cooking. Then both serve in a relaxed manner, enjoying conversation with your friends.

If you feel insecure about the way you cook, the way you serve, or about the topics of conversation, then you are judging yourself, or feel that other people are judging you, or both. You can improve your entertaining style by learning the arts of cooking simple and attractive meals, or by accepting what you do and the way you do it. Or, if you simply dislike entertaining at home, there is no reason why you must do it. Just be sure that you both agree on what you are willing, and wish, to do.

b. Get-togethers for bridge or music.

c. Potlucks: Many women prefer to invite their friends for potlucks or gourmet lunches. It saves time and creates a cooperative effort. The shared responsibility also makes the entertainment easier for everyone.

d. Seeing home movies.

e. Going out to dinner or the theater.

Many other choices are open to you, of course, but the important thing is that you and your partner should agree on how you wish to spend time with your friends. Negotiate so that you're both satisfied.

4. How large a circle of friends do you need as a couple?

How many friendships can you maintain? Perhaps you need only four or five close friends or couples, while you consider others acquaintances. How many friends do each of you require outside of your relationship?

5. Who are your most significant friends, and how much time do you wish to spend with them?

6. Do you choose to see friends always as a couple, or can you maintain close friendships on your own without sharing them with your partner?

7. What do you do if you only enjoy the company of one person from a couple? Do you try to see just that person, or forget about the friendship altogether?

8. How do you and your partner handle separate interests?

Suppose you like to play golf and your partner doesn't, while she likes concerts but you don't. Does

Managing Friendships

she suffer along playing golf with you, while you allow yourself to be dragged to concerts? Or do you give up golf and concerts? Or do you allow each other to find outside friends with whom to share these individual interests?

9. Will you allow each other to have friends of the opposite sex, whose friendship you do not share?

This is a big question, but one you can answer if you are open and honest with each other. However, it opens other questions, such as, can you trust yourself and each other to keep such a friendship within agreed-upon bounds? Will you set limitations such as, it's okay to meet during the day and in public but not alone, either day or night?

10. How far can you respect each other's "space" and need for freedom? Is your love and trust for each other deep enough to cope with an outside affair, if that should develop from a friendship? Be *very* sure that you and your partner understand and *agree* with each other on this question, realizing that it is difficult to cultivate an opposite-sex friendship without sexual overtones.

11. How do you resolve past hurts if the freedom was misused and the trust betrayed?

Can you forgive, forget, and start with a new full trust dealing only with the present?

12. What does intimacy mean to each of you? How much intimacy do you need? How much of this need is filled through each other? How much of this need will you allow each other to fulfill through outside friendships?

Be honest with yourself and your partner. If the intimacy you need from friends is greater than you derive from your partner, then perhaps you need to reexamine the basis of your relationship.

Whether we like it or not, friendships involve emotions and it is not always possible to dictate coolly and rationally the course of a friendship. Yet, virtually every person needs friends no matter how fulfilling a marriage or other intimate relationship may be. However, if you are aware of the rewards as well as the dangers of friendship and manage friendships accordingly, you can go far in forestalling problems in your relationship.

12
The Art of Negotiating Contracts

As we've seen throughout this book, the most important skill two individuals can use to make a relationship successful is the art of negotiating.

The word "contract" may seem to be a cold and rigid way to express the physical, mental, and emotional closeness of a marital relationship. Yet, we live each day of our lives responding to written or unwritten contracts, either abiding by them or violating them.

Each time you stop your car at a stop light you fulfill a contract to protect your safety and that of others. Each morning when you get out of bed and get to work on time, you are fulfilling a contract with your employer and more importantly, with your partner to whom you have committed an expenditure of time and energy to insure your financial security together. Whenever you cook breakfast or mow the lawn, you are fulfilling a piece of the contract with your partner.

A contract, therefore, is nothing more than a clear

presentation of the commitments two people make to each other. If you and your partner have worked together through the preceding chapters of this book, you have already gained awareness and sensitivity to problem areas in your relationship. We've seen how in many, if not all, cases being able to compromise is the only way to avoid crisis. But in order to compromise, you both must have a clear understanding of what the "rules" of your relationship are, what's important to both of you, and where you can and cannot compromise. It is for this reason—even though you may have been living according to unwritten rules between you—that we recommend that you write a specific contract governing your relationship and then renew and rewrite it at regular intervals.

Marriage Vows

Isn't love enough? Aren't our marriage vows enough?

The answer is *no*. Love is not enough to account for individual differences and needs. Marriage vows are not enough because, even though they may be "binding" in a civil or religious sense, the marriage ritual was designed to cover general situations and again does not consider individual differences and needs.

Consider for a moment what we pledge to do during the marriage ceremony. We vow "to have and to hold, to cherish, and, in some cases, obey, for better or for worse." These are beautiful and valid vows, but what do they mean in terms of day-to-day living? What does it mean for you, two individuals, to have and to hold? How firmly do you hold? Who obeys whom? Does for better or for worse mean that you must cling to each other no matter how bad your relationship may become?

Unfortunately, many of the answers to these questions

are not clear until couples reach the divorce courts. There's no telling how many relationships might have been saved by realistic marriage contracts, but I do know that I've used the approach successfully with hundreds of couples. For a number of years, I have guided couples, who had been married from one year to thirty, in writing marriage contracts. Many of these faced a crisis that had only two solutions: dissolving their marriage, or trying to straighten out their problems and establishing healthier patterns.

These individuals were not looking for prolonged, in-depth counseling. They were hurting and needed a direct approach—guidance in dealing with their *present* hurts. They needed to evaluate their relationships and arrive at marriage contracts which accounted for, and provided for, their *separate* needs and their *combined* needs. A new marriage contract, as many of them found, can mark the rebirth of a relationship.

Other couples see the marriage contract as a tool for enhancing an already healthy and happy marriage. Thus, marriage enrichment is another goal for writing such a contract. Marriages need renewal and enrichment just as soil needs organic material added each season to insure a healthier bloom.

Ideally, a detailed marriage contract should be written and then reviewed under the following conditions:

1. *Before* marriage.
2. Periodically—perhaps once a year—after marriage, to determine if the contract is fulfilling the needs and desires of both partners. Make it part of your anniversary celebration.
3. Whenever problems arise and before crises occur.

An important fact to remember is that *it is never too late in a marriage to write a contract for enrichment or problem solving.*

How Do We Start?

Let us suppose you are contemplating marriage. What do you and your proposed partner need to know about yourselves as individuals, and about each other, in order to create a sound and comprehensive contract?

First, you must examine yourself—knowing and defining one's dreams, expectations, ambitions, emotions, strengths and weaknesses, one's mind, body, and feelings, is necessary. Remember, a contract is a commitment. It is an agreement between two people to do something to and for each other. To do this, each must know what his or her own needs are. In a marriage, the partners choose to live together and share their lives because this seems to offer the greatest rewards for them. What makes it rewarding is the balance of freedom, the commitment they accept, and the personal needs which they fulfill for their partner and themselves.

As a first step, compare your life alone with the life you anticipate with your partner. Or, if you are already living in an intimate relationship, recall those areas which you found satisfying while living alone along with those in which you needed to share with someone else for fulfillment.

Use your workbook and ask yourself "When I was living alone, what were my ten most important needs?"

List anything that comes to mind. Write your answers spontaneously. List more than ten if you can. Here are some examples:

A neat apartment
Books and records
Personal freedom
Friends
Nice clothes
A satisfying job
Financial independence

A constant companion
A lover
Physical comfort
Parties
Attending sports events
Participating in sports
Attending the theater
Vacationing in the snow
A balanced diet
Regular exercise
Soaking in a hot tub
Talking on the phone
Playing cards and games

Remember, this is your personal list. It helps to identify you to your partner. Some of the above items may fit you, while others do not. Once you have completed this list, rearrange the items in order of importance to you and compare them with your partner's list.

Once you have completed this part of the exercise, answer the question, "What are the ten most important things I want from an intimate relationship or marriage?"

Love
Companionship
Understanding
Support
Caring and comfort
Friendship
Intellectual challenge
Emotional closeness
Physical closeness
Sex
Sharing a home
Having children
Trust

Commitment
Travel together
Escape from loneliness
Partner as adviser
Partner as confidante

Again, do not be confined to these. When you are finished, list the top ten needs and desires in order of importance. This list may include some items from your first list but note, of course, that there are certain things you can have with a partner but not when you are alone. Also, you may note that the opposite is true—that marriage may limit the satisfaction of some needs and freedoms that you've enjoyed as a single person. In comparing the second list with the first list, you and your partner will learn what is most important to each of you, and begin to measure—realistically—what you are capable of providing for each other. If you are already married, this comparison may reveal areas of need which you are *not* satisfying for your partner, or vice versa. It may also be the first time you are aware of certain wishes and desires. As we have said repeatedly, your partner may not be aware of your needs unless you express them, and you can't ask if you don't know your own needs.

Throughout this preliminary examination, which will lead to your marriage contract, you are teaching yourself to think in specific terms rather than vague generalities so that you learn what you may expect of each other. Again using your workbook, you can refine the process further by asking yourself the following questions.

1. What will make me happy?
Is it money or possessions? Is it undying love and devotion? Is it children? Is it security? Or is it a combination of these with other things? Answer as explicitly as you can.

The Art of Negotiating Contracts

2. What are my dreams and fantasies?

Do I imagine my husband to be a masterful lover who carries me away to a life of ease and luxury, or do I dream of an ordinary man with whom to share whatever life has to offer? Do I dream of a gorgeous but virtuous wife envied by all the men around me, or a woman who will walk with me steadfastly through triumphs and failures? What is *your* dream?

3. What do I want to have in a year, five years, ten years, twenty years, from now?

For most of us, it is a big order to set goal this far in the future, but you will deepen and broaden your understanding of each other by setting down your thoughts on this. Do you want to own a home, have healthy children? Do you want to be a successful doctor or lawyer? Do you want to be a highly successful career woman with children, without children, before or after having children? Each of you may spend an entire evening answering this question.

4. What are my ambitions as an individual?

To be a great surgeon? An operatic soprano? President of a corporation or home decorating agency? . . . as part of a couple? To be a good father or mother? Sharing in the care of our home and family?

For us as a couple? To be comfortably wealthy? To enjoy travel and many friends? To be widely respected in our community?

5. What are my strengths and what are my weaknesses?

6. What are my partner's strengths and weaknesses?

These last two are difficult questions to answer and we have not suggested answers because this is a very personal matter between you and your partner. Needless to say, it is necessary to answer both questions fully and honestly if you are to come to a realistic marriage contract. Once you've answered these questions you'll be able to see clearly where the two of you may not be seeing eye-to-eye and where you are.

The final step in your individual examinations is to answer the following questions.

1. Who are we as a unit?
2. What are our strengths and weaknesses as a couple?
3. What are our individual needs?

After you've answered these questions separately, compare your answers. How are they similar and different? Where differences exist, do you see ways in which you can compromise?

This is the heart of your marriage contract—full clarification of your needs and full understanding of what you can and cannot fulfill for your partner. For example, if he asks for your lifelong promise of fidelity and emotional security, can you honestly commit yourself in writing to provide these to him or her? If not, what are the limitations on your commitment. Can you promise these things for a year? If so, write it that way in the contract, with an option to renew that promise or renegotiate it at the end of the year. If he is unsure that he can provide one of your deepest needs—financial security—perhaps you can negotiate this point. Perhaps the contract clause will say that you promise to work *together* toward financial security.

In this fashion, work down through your lists of essential needs, and write each of your small agreements into the larger one.

At this point you are probably emotionally exhausted, but you will have cleared away much of the ambiguity and false romantic pictures you may have made of your love and marriage. Your steps toward negotiations for a contract should be a fair and realistic representation of what you—

as two individuals—can do for each other in your intimate relationship.

Now, also, it is perhaps safe to tell you that you've covered the most difficult part. You've dealt with the deepest emotional needs. Now you can move on to a series of mini- or sub-contracts dealing with the day-to-day issues of life. Write agreements to cover at least the following:

1. Money
2. Household management
3. Children
4. Friends and social activities
5. Recreation and vacations
6. Professional life

Money

Here are some points to cover on the question of money.

1. Will one person or both be responsible for earning?
2. Will one person control how the money is spent, or will this be handled by joint agreement?
3. Does one of you want to be responsible for bill-paying and handling the checkbook, or will you take turns handling this monthly chore?
4. Will you combine your incomes, or keep separate accounts?
5. Will one or both of you handle budgeting problems?
6. Will one of you receive a weekly or monthly allowance from the paycheck or will you decide upon expenditures jointly? Will each of you have freedom to

spend minor amounts of money without accounting to the other? What limits will you set?

Resolve your money issues into a mini-contract before moving on to the next issue. It doesn't matter in what form your contract is written. Use your own language, your own words. Just begin by saying that you two agree to the following, and make sure you both sign all contracts and their renewals and even have witnesses if you feel it will help "legitimize" the contract for you both.

Household Management

There are really two parts to this mini-contract: (1) your place and style of living, and (2) responsibility for household management and work. Following are some questions to help you get started.

1. If you had a free choice, where would you want to live? A cabin in the hills? A house in the suburbs? An apartment in the city?
2. In the home of your choice, does each of you need separate rooms to insure private space for those times when you need to be apart?
3. Do you want a small, cozy dwelling or a large ostentatious house with expensive furniture?
4. Do you want to care for a large lawn with trees and flowers or are these things unimportant to you?
5. When it comes to household work, will you cling to the traditional male-female roles in which the woman does all the cooking and housework, or will you share these duties?
6. Will you take turns washing dishes and laundry?
7. Will you take turns cleaning house, or find a division of duties acceptable to both of you? (For ex-

The Art of Negotiating Contracts

ample, perhaps the husband does not mind cleaning bathrooms while his wife prefers to do the vacuuming.)

8. Will one or both of you be responsible for yard work?

9. Will one or both of you be responsible for automobile maintenance?

Children

Again, this is a two-part contract: (1) Will we have children, and (2) if so, how will we share child-care duties?

In deciding the question of whether or not to have children, refer to the earlier chapter on this subject. The contract must deal with the professional ambitions of both partners, particularly the woman's because she is the one who must cope with pregnancy.

You may decide that you want many children, or none.

If you want children without interrupting the wife's study or professional career, you may decide to adopt.

If both of you are sure you want at least one child but are uncertain of your parental capabilities to handle more than that, you may agree to have one baby (assuming, of course, that this is possible), and then renegotiate the contract after that baby is born.

Once you come to agreement on having children, the next step is to negotiate a contract detailing the duties of child-care. Some questions to consider are:

1. Will mother be entirely responsible for child-care, diaper washing, and training until the child reaches preschool age, or will father share in these duties?

2. Will one parent be the disciplinarian or will both share this duty? (Remember our discussion of the importance of a united front.)

3. Who will get up in the night for feedings or to comfort a child who is ill? Will you alternate?

You may have every good intention of sharing fully in these matters, but it is important to write down as many details as possible in your contract *before* you embark upon parenthood.

Friends and Social Activities

Referring again to previous chapters, carefully consider your needs and wishes in this realm, and then write down your agreements and compromises.

1. Will you agree to accept each other's friends freely and completely?
2. Will you give each other freedom to spend some time alone with your particular friends?
3. Will you be jealous of opposite-sex friendships?
4. How far are you willing to trust your partner in opposite-sex friendships?
5. What types of recreation do each of you prefer? Sports? Theater? Dinner parties? Drinking and dancing?
6. Can you agree to share all of these with each other, or enjoy some of them alone or with other friends?
7. Will you take an extended vacation every year, or break up your vacations into smaller segments, such as weekends?
8. Where do you prefer to vacation? The beach? Camping? The mountains? Visiting historic sites? If your tastes differ, your contract should contain an agreement as to how you will divide up these activities.
9. Do you enjoy quiet and relaxation when you go

away, or the social whirl and excitement of resort centers? Again, find a balance between your wishes.

Professional Life

A most vital mini-contract, as part of your overall marriage contract, is that dealing with your professional ambitions and those of your partner.

> 1. If your husband has political ambitions, can you enjoy moving in his shadow and even helping him to attain office? If you can, or cannot, say so clearly.
> 2. Do you object to your wife working outside the home?
> 3. Do you object to her studying for advanced professional degrees and subsequent practice?
> 4. Can you give each other complete freedom to follow your own professional aspirations?

These questions should be clearly and pragmatically answered in the premarital contract, and then renegotiated periodically if and when conflicts arise.

Go through all of the areas we've focused on in this book, and cover them in mini-contracts. You can negotiate about your families, about communication (How much is enough? Should we set aside time? etc.), about time, intimacy, in fact, any aspect of your marriage that you both feel should be spelled out and defined in this manner.

The Broken Contract

Considering the many points and complexities you've worked through by this time, it would be a miracle if a contract were carried out to the precise letter. As circumstances and feelings change, it may become undesirable or impossible for one or both of you to do some of the things you promised. When a contract has been broken, you need to examine the terms of the agreement again and ask yourselves some questions. Your by now dog-eared workbook can play an important role again.

- Why wasn't the commitment kept?
- How do you feel about the broken commitment?
- How does your partner feel about the broken commitment?
- How can you revise the contract to make it more realistic in current terms?
- How will you deal with the situation if the same commitment is broken again?

You may agree that if any part of the contract is not workable for either of you, you will renegotiate that part rather than continue with a breach of contract. For instance:

Your husband has promised to help you each evening in the kitchen, to share the task of bathing the children and putting them to bed, and to help with regular household chores. After a month, he finds he is too tired after work to share these responsibilities with you.

At this point, renegotiate the division of responsibilities. If he is tired occasionally, you can take over his duties now and then. If he is *always* tired, maybe you can trade jobs. Perhaps he can handle morning rather than evening chores. Perhaps he can prepare lunches for the children and get them off to school.

An equitable arrangement almost always can be found if both partners are willing to compromise. If they are not, the marriage contract will not work.

Including the Children

As your children grow old enough to express their needs and wishes clearly, they should be included in a family contract. Every three months, for example, you may have a family meeting over your contract and ask the children:
What do you need?
What do you want?
What are your goals and dreams?
Such questions need to be broken down into simple specifics, of course, depending upon the age of the children. Some answers might include:

1. I need a new bicycle to ride to school.
2. I'd like to go out for football and have you come see the games.
3. I would like to have an hour of games with you every night.
4. I'd like to go to the zoo or out for a walk with only one of you at a time.
5. I'd like to spend the summer at a lake and learn how to water ski.

Individual wishes and needs must be knit by compromise into the overall fabric of the family, considering time and economic limitations as well as others. The children must understand and accept these limitations as well as what they agree to do on their side of the contract. This is an ideal area to set up agreements on family chores, allowances, bed time, and homework.

Yes, writing the marriage contract is work. Yes, enriching a dull marriage is work. But most good things in life do require work and attention and what can be more worthwhile than a warm, lasting, intimate relationship.

I would only hope that you will still be rewriting your marriage contract on your fiftieth anniversary and beyond.

13
What to Do When It Doesn't Work

It would be pleasant if you could ignore this chapter, if you could say that your working through previous chapters had solved all the problems in your relationship. However, as we have impressed upon you the necessity for practical realism in marriage, it is only realistic to consider what steps and actions remain for you if you have worked through the book without success. You've read the book. You've done the exercises. Yet you have been unable to resolve some basic conflicts with your partner.

You may feel hopeless about this, or you may feel panicky, aware that you have come to a major crisis. The illness of marriage can be just as real as illness of the body. At the onset, you apply home remedies. But if fever rises too far, you know you are dealing with a serious infection and you call the doctor. Your marriage, just as your body, contains remarkable healing power, but if you have done everything you can by yourself, it may be time for you to seek the professional services of an impartial third party.

What to Do When It Doesn't Work

The marriage counselor is like a marriage doctor, there to listen, guide, and help you to pull yourselves through the painful areas of your relationship.

Before you begin searching for that special third person to help you, however, now is the time to make one last major effort between yourselves.

Did the exercises fail completely, or were there some areas in which you were able to improve relations?

Why didn't the exercises work for you?

Was it because one of you refused (or was unable) to open completely to the other?

Both of you must answer this last question honestly. It is crucial to the entire process of reconciliation and refreshment of a relationship. Both of you participated wholeheartedly when the relationship began; you must both participate openly to keep it alive. The finest therapist in the world cannot help you unless each of you is willing to look inside yourselves, to do some soul searching, to experience some pain, to be willing to *change* and *grow*. You must both be open to new thoughts, new ways of looking at things. Without this openness, you may as well save yourselves the time and money involved in outside counseling.

Also, before you hasten to the therapist, consider the possibility that the lessons of this book *have been* working for you even though your relationship now may seem more confused and difficult than it was before you started. The fact is, things very often *get worse before they get better*. The reason this is true is that as you worked—openly and diligently—through the exercises, you undoubtedly peeled away scar tissue from some old wounds, hurts, and conflicts, long hidden behind silence because you felt it was hopeless to try to accomplish anything. Now you have reopened these old areas of vulnerability and stand exposed before each other. You may like what you see, or you may not. You may be willing to remain open and vulnerable, or you may feel an overwhelming urge to hide again—to return to that dull, gray level of superficial living which, although it was not very pleasant, at least it did not hurt violently.

Now you are at the crisis point, beyond which either your relationship will be enriched and renewed, or else you may be forced to end it to benefit the two individuals involved.

Crisis Management

Crises, either specific or general, often lead to better relationships. In Chinese, crisis has two meanings—danger and opportunity for change. In this case, the danger may be dissolution of a marriage. The change is a new beginning. It is the ability to admit that the old marriage is dead, the old relationship cannot exist any longer. You have arrived at a point where either there is mutual readiness to start a new relationship with the *same* person, or there is total disagreement and the marriage must be dissolved. Is it more important to save this marriage, or to cling to your old attitudes and feelings?

Here is an example in which a general marital crisis led to positive change.

Jim and Ann fought about nearly everything. Ann was an artist and also taught in a local college. Jim was involved in computer design, and in the evenings was too tired and impatient to listen to Ann's stories about her work. Ann felt that Jim did not respect her and did not appreciate her work and her world of art.

Jim was angry each time he came home and found the house untidy. He freely vented his unhappiness that she spent time in front of the easel instead of behind a vacuum cleaner. He was equally impatient with Ann's barking dog (which she loved as if it were her child), and resented her long telephone conversations with friends.

What to Do When It Doesn't Work

Although these superficial points of friction may have been no more than symptoms of deeper conflict, Ann finally decided she could not absorb Jim's constant criticism any longer. She could not tolerate the limits on her freedom to talk with friends and to be herself. She announced she was moving out.

Jim was shocked into reexamining himself and their relationship. He finally recognized the depth of Ann's unhappiness and, using the skills he had as an analytical engineer, tried to work through the logic of their crisis. First, he concluded that it was more important to him to be married than to be separated. Then, as they worked their way through several stormy arguments and discussions, he saw that his basic anger and frustration were not aimed at Ann, but rather toward the people for whom he worked. He was bored in his work and felt trapped. Instead of doing something about *that,* he vented his criticism on his wife when he came home to find untidiness and turmoil rather than the solace and quiet he needed from her. They both learned something from this interchange.

Jim realized he had been unfair in his bitter criticism of his wife and Ann learned that *he* needed *her,* something that had not been clear before. He began to show more kindness to her, to take more interest in her work, to allow her more space in which to relate to friends, to talk more with her about the things that were disturbing him. Ann also learned to listen, but most of all she learned to assert herself when Jim was angry and not to feel responsible for his outbursts of anger.

For these two, the crisis was the beginning of new communication. They learned to share joys and frustrations, their trials and triumphs with each other each day. Instead of splitting apart in anger, they came together in mutual support. The crisis served to bring them closer together.

The major crisis, of course, does not always have a happy ending. It always has its two sides, danger and opportunity. But if all other avenues have been exploited, the crisis can at least lead you to a clear-cut solution. Let's consider a severe and fundamental hypothetical situation, a specific crisis which often destroys marriages.

The wife believes her husband has been having a love affair with another woman (it could be the other way around, of course). Her evidence is circumstantial. He seems cool and distant and avoids intimate moments with her. He has been spending considerable time away from home in the evenings because his office work has piled up. Her friends told her they had seen her husband having lunch with his secretary. He is often curt and short-tempered with his wife.

She is tortured by the almost sure knowledge that her marriage is slipping into disaster, yet she is fearful that if she confronts her husband with accusations, she will precipitate an immediate break in their relationship. She cannot tolerate the thought that he is sleeping with another woman, but dreads the moment when she will know for sure.

Finally, this wife realizes that she has nothing more to lose, and demands an answer.

"Are you having an affair with Jennifer?" she asks her husband. "Please don't lie to me. I've got to know."

Her husband looks at her in surprise and annoyance.

"No, I'm not," he says. "What makes you think that?"

His wife tells him of the circumstantial evidence that she has accumulated against him.

"I don't think I've ever lied to you," her husband says, "and I'm not lying now. I've never had an affair with Jennifer or anyone else. I've been under a lot of pressure at work lately, but I can account for every hour I've been away from you."

At this point, his wife has several choices. She can accept his word in trust, and attempt to work with him in bringing new closeness into their relationship. She can demand more proof, indicating to him that she *does not* trust him. She can accept the fact that the entire episode was her imagination. Or she can continue to be suspicious. If she chooses the course of continuing suspicion, however, she must realize that this is *her* problem. In any case, she has these many choices of procedure after the crisis.

Now let us suppose that her husband *was* having an affair. Their marriage had been growing dull and uninteresting and he was tempted to find new levels of satisfaction with another woman. At the same time, he recognizes that his relationship with his wife is so shaky that there is little more to lose. The crisis is the time to reveal all secrets.

"Yes," he says, "I have been having an affair with her. It really didn't mean much to me and it's over now. I didn't tell you before because I was afraid you'd leave me. I'm sorry, and if you'll forgive me, I want our marriage to continue on a better plane."

Both partners now have a different set of decisions to make. She can forgive and they can rebuild new sensitivity to each other on waves of forgiveness. Or she can hold him by force of guilt, saying, "I'll forgive you this time but if you ever stray again, our marriage is over." Or she can decide that betrayal is no basis for a marriage and leave him. Once crisis has opened channels of communication, they can decide if it is more satisfying to cling to old negative feelings, or to move forward into a new form of their partnership.

As you can see, crisis—either one that comes from knowing that you have come to the end of your rope and haven't solved the problems or one that comes about from a specific incident—can push you both to go the extra distance, to try that much harder to make your relationship work. What you both must decide is, "Do you want to stay married?" If the answer is yes, open all channels of communication. Try these exercises before going further for help.

1. Be honest with yourself. Be willing to risk baring your most difficult feelings about your partner, but without judgment.
2. Express your feelings about your relationship. Write them down in your workbook:

>I am bored.
>I feel used.
>I feel lonely.
>I need more attention.
>I need your undivided love.
>I need closeness.
>I need a time and place to communicate.

Continue your list and then compare it with your partner's. Read your partner's list, then ask yourself if and then how you can meet most of his or her needs.
3. Ask yourselves:
>"How long ago did I notice the break in our communications?"
>
>"What am I doing to try to improve our communications?" If the answer is "Nothing," ask yourself, "What is preventing it?"

Ask yourself the question asked in the beginning of the book,
>"Are you willing to work to improve the relationship?"
>
>"Is your partner willing?"

If the answers are "yes," then make a commitment to take prime time each day to talk about your feelings and unfulfilled needs. Listen *without* arguing and deal with one issue at a time.

For example, your partner says that there is no closeness, no attraction between you anymore. He says you now have little in common and he is bored. These all seem like loaded statements, and they are! You have to work with them one at a time and gently defuse them. You might not know where to start, but agree to negotiate and discuss *one issue at a time*.

At first, talk only about the statement, "There is no feeling of closeness between us anymore." Presume that both of you agree. Ask yourself, "How does it feel when you are closer? What do you think about your partner when you think 'close' thoughts?" Write a list of positive thoughts and feelings which make you feel close again, such as:

When you pay attention to my needs, I feel close.
When we make love, I feel close.
When you praise and nurture me, I feel close.

After writing all the statements you can think of, ask each other, "Can we pay more attention to each other's needs? Do we *want* to?"

Remember—if you want to, and decide to do it, you can.

What we have been encouraging you to learn throughout this book is:

1. Ask new questions.
2. Change your old responses to situations.
3. Think positively and constructively.

Ask yourself, "How can I do it better now?" Write down and role play a new you. If you have done this diligently and together, throughout the book, at least half of your large and small problems should be in the process of solution. If you try but can't resolve a certain problem, don't give up. Try again by feeding positive statements to each other in "I" messages like the following.
- I love being close to you.
- I love for you to touch me.
- I like the warmth and security I get from you.

- I sense a wall between us.
- I don't know how to break through to you.

The Problems You Can't Solve

Some of you will be fortunate enough to solve all your problems on your own. However, if you have really tried and find that you still need help, look for a counselor. It is important to work with a person who believes in treating the relationship as well as both of you as individuals.

In the past, counseling was done for the most part by relatives, physicians, and clergymen. The value of these counselors was their willingness to listen, their acceptance and empathy without the compulsion to pass judgment. Many of these qualities are therapeutic and helpful. Actually, the worst modern-day counselor is the one who has all the answers and tries to manipulate you or convince you that there is one right answer for you. All the sources which were the only ones available in the past are still valuable today. If you have a caring friend who is a good listener, and whom you could trust, use him or her as a sounding board. A close relative or your minister may serve the same function. Finally, if you still feel there are areas in your relationship that are nearly gone but worth saving, seek a professional counselor.

How Long Should We Struggle?

This is an important question, which many ask as they experience the pain of trying to change their relationship. When is a marriage dead? Let's face it, no matter how hard they struggle, some couples are simply not meant to live with each other. After you have made every possible effort to save your marriage, you will know when it is over.

Dissolving a bad relationship (just as working to save a good one) demands courage and honesty with yourself and your spouse. Two people who have self-esteem and are assertive should have the courage to admit that they like themselves individually but just not with each other. They can realize that they *both* deserve a better relationship. As with the death of a dear one, we mourn the death of marriage, we experience the loss and we learn to accept the reality of it. But life is limited. Some relationships are likewise limited and their life cycle comes to an end.

If divorce finally turns out to be the best solution for you, it is important not to view it as a failure. Rather, view it as a creative step with the full knowledge that you tried to work on your marriage with each other, and with a competent marriage counselor, and yet you and your partner remain unhappy. The marriage is dead.

Once this relationship has finally ended, it is also important for you to know that a new relationship can be a rebirth. The important thing is to learn from the past experience and not to jump into another just like it. You learned—the first time around—how to use the skills outlined in this book. Now use it again as you stand on the threshold of a new relationship.

You Made It

Some of you—we hope *most* of you—found new plateaus of loving and marriage enrichment as you labored through the exercises in this book. In one chapter, you gave yourselves a marital check-up. Now ask yourselves these same questions again and have a dialogue with your partner.

1. Have we resolved any disagreements?
2. Have we improved our relationship?
3. Are we now able to argue constructively about our relations, and make changes where they are necessary?

And now, one final notation for your workbook.
Write the following in a love letter to each other.
"I resolve to repeat our marital check-up at least twice each year, and review our marriage contracts. If provisions have been broken, or circumstances have changed, I further resolve to work with you in rewriting our contracts so that our marriage will remain rich and alive for all of our days."
We could wish you nothing better than that.

Bibliography

Bach, Dr. George R., and Wyden, Peter. *The Intimate Enemy: How to Fight Fair in Love and Marriage.* New York: William Morrow & Co., 1969.

Baer, Jean. *How to Be an Assertive (Not Aggressive) Woman.* New York: Rawson Associates Publishers, Inc., 1976.

Barbach, Lonnie Garfield. *For Yourself: The Fulfillment of Female Sexuality.* Garden City, New York: Doubleday & Co., 1975.

Belliveau, Fred, and Richter, Lin. *Understanding Human Sexual Inadequacy.* New York: Bantam, 1970.

Bower, Sharon Anthony, and Bower, Gordon H. *Asserting Yourself: A Practical Guide for Positive Change.* Menlo Park, California: Addison-Wesley Publishing Co., 1976.

Charny, Israel, M.D. *Marital Love and Hate.* New York: Macmillan Publishing Co., Inc., 1972.

Eichenlaub, John E., M.D. *The Marriage Art.* New York: Dell Publishing Co., Inc., 1961.

BIBLIOGRAPHY

Fabry, Joseph B. *The Pursuit of Meaning.* Boston: Beacon Press, 1968.

Friday, Nancy. *My Secret Garden.* New York: Simon & Schuster, 1974.

Gordon, Thomas. *P.E.T. Parent Effectiveness Training.* New York: Peter H. Wyden, Inc., 1970.

Greenwald, Jerry, M.D. *Creative Intimacy: How to Break the Patterns that Poison Your Relationships.* New York: Simon & Schuster, 1975.

Hite, Shere. *The Hite Report, a Nationwide Study of Female Sexuality.* New York: Macmillan Publishing Co., Inc., 1976.

Keyes, Margaret Frings. *Staying Married.* Millbrae, California: Les Femmes, 1975.

Koestenbaum, Peter. *Existential Sexuality; Choosing to Love.* Englewood Cliffs, New Jersey: Prentice-Hall, Inc., 1974.

Koestenbaum, Peter. *Managing Anxiety: The Power of Knowing Who You Are.* Englewood Cliffs, New Jersey: Prentice-Hall, Inc., 1974.

Krantzler, Mel. *Creative Divorce.* New York: M. Evans & Company, 1973.

Lakein, Alan. *How to Get Control of Your Time and Your Life.* New York: Peter H. Wyden, Inc., 1973.

Lederer, William J., and Jackson, Don D., M.D. *The Mirages of Marriage.* New York: W.W. Norton & Co., 1968.

Luthman, Shirley Gehrke, with Kirschenbaum, Martin. *The Dynamic Family.* Palo Alto, California: Science and Behavior Books, Inc., 1974.

Masters, William H., and Johnson, Virginia E. *The Pleasure Bond.* Boston: Little, Brown & Co., 1970.

Miller, Sherod; Nunnally, Elam W.; and Wackman, Daniel B. *Alive and Aware: Improving Communication in Relation-*

Bibliography

ships. Minneapolis, Minnesota: Interpersonal Communication Programs, Inc., 1975.

Nierenberg, Gerard I. *The Art of Negotiating*. New York: Cornerstone Library, 1968.

Satir, Virginia. *Peoplemaking*. Palo Alto, California: Science and Behavior Books, Inc., 1972.

Shostrom, Everett L. *Man, the Manipulator*. New York: Abingdon-Bantam, 1967.

Shostrom, Everett L., and Kavanaugh, James. *Between Man & Woman*. New York: Bantam Books, 1972.

Simon, Sidney H.; Howe, Leland W.; and Kirschenbaum, Howard. *Values Clarification, A Handbook of Practical Strategies for Teachers and Students*. New York: Hart Publishing Co., Inc., 1972.

Smith, Gerald Walker, with Phillips, Alice I. *Me, You and Us*. New York: Peter H. Wyden, Inc., 1971.

Suid, Roberta; Bradley, Buff; Suid, Murray; and Eastman, Jean. *Married, Etc*. Menlo Park, California: Addison-Wesley, 1976.

Van Caspel, Venita. *Money Dynamics*. Reston, Virginia: Reston Publishing Co., Inc., 1975.

Index

Bach, George, 99–100, 102
   and Wyden, Peter, *The Intimate Enemy: Creative Aggression*, 55
body language, 83, 87, 90, 92–93, 138

case histories:
   children, 201–2, 203
   communication, 87, 88–90
   crisis management, 253–55
   family relationship problems, 168–69
   friends and friendship, 226–27
   fulfilled marriage, 42–43
   "love conquers all" myth, 6–7
   marriage myths and realities, 32–34
   money, 174–75, 182–83, 184–85, 186–88
   outside activities, 171–73
   self-disclosure, 60
   self-liking, 64–65
   sexual differences, 128
   "sexual perfection" myth, 7–8
   time use, 159–60, 162
   values, 140–41, 146–47, 148–49
   weight problems, 84–85, 148–49
children, 191–218
   assertiveness with, 207, 209–10, 211
   case histories, 201–2, 203
   child care roles, 200–1
   contracts about, 243, 245–46
   contracts with, 207, 212, 249
   cooperation of, 207, 208–9
   disagreement about having, 198–200
   discipline of, 205–6, 207
   empty-nest syndrome, 215–17

Index

children (*Continued*)
  expectations about, 193–94, 213
  family meetings with, 207, 210–11
  father's jealousy of, 201–2
  grown, 217–18
  intimacy necessary despite, 203–4
  jealousy of, 204
  letting go of, 214–15
  motivations in having, 192–93
  needs of, 204
  pain and disappointment with, 213
  parental rescue of, 213–14
  premarital agreement on, 192, 194, 199–200
  problem-solving of, 213–14
  questions for men, 193, 194–95
  questions for women, 193, 194
  reasons for having, 196, 197
  reasons for not having, 197–98
  responsibilities of, 207–12
  special problems with, 213
  united front necessary with, 205–6, 245
communication, 61–62, 65, 83–94
  body language in, 83, 87, 90, 92–93
  case histories, 87, 88–90
  exercises, 76–77, 91–94, 136–37
  honesty in, 88–90
  levels of, 93–94
  listening as, 90
  nonjudgmental, 90–91
  self-assertion in, 88
  self-awareness and self-knowledge in, 58–61, 83–84, 85–87

  sex-related, 132–33, 136
  silence as, 91–92
conflicts and conflict resolution, 11–12, 27–28, 30, 32, 94–109, 186
  See also Contracts and contract negotiating
contracts and contract negotiating, 235–49
  broken, 247–48
  on children, 243, 245–46
  children included in, 249
  coverage of, 243–47
  defined, 235–36
  exercises, 238–41, 242
  on friends and social activities, 243, 246–47
  on household management, 243, 244–45
  importance of, 235, 249
  marriage vows as, 236–37
  on money, 243–44
  on professional life, 243, 247
  on recreation and vacations, 243
  renegotiation of, 248
  review of, 237, 249, 260
  as tool for enrichment, 237
  unwritten, 235
  See also Conflicts and conflict resolution; Minicontracts

divorce, 3, 10, 12, 14, 17, 115, 237
  as creative step, 259
  emotional, 105–7

emotional divorce, 105–7
empty-nest syndrome, 215–17
exercises:
  boredom avoidance, 138–39
  children, 193, 194–95, 196, 218
  conflict summary, 80–81
  contracts and contract ne-

INDEX

exercises (*Continued*)
  gotiating, 238–41, 243
  crisis management, 255–58
  dyadic adjustment scale, 65–66
  family relationships, 167–68, 169–70
  fight inventory, 100–101
  final, 259–60
  friends and friendships, 223, 224–25, 228–29, 230–33
  interpersonal comparison, 69–73
  intimacy, 130–32, 135–36
  listening, 73–74
  marital appraisal, 67–69
  marriage myths and realities, 25–29, 34–37
  marriage style evaluation, 50–53
  mini-contracts, 29–31, 188
  money, 185–86
  negotiating resolutions, 95–99
  relaxation, 57
  role reversal in, 24, 73–74, 97–98
  self-disclosure, 58–61
  self-liking, 61–65
  sex, 78–80, 117, 126–27, 129, 134–37
  success of, 251
  taking directions, 73–74
  time priorities, management and use, 77–78, 157–59, 161–62
  trivial irritations, 23–24
  values and value conflicts, 143–46, 154
  yes–no inventory, 75–76
extramarital relationships, 44–46, 115, 124–26, 254–55

family meetings, 207, 210–11
fighting, 11–12, 100–109
  avoidance of, 104–5
  as catharsis, 101–2

constructive, 100
distance in, 102–3
and emotional divorce, 105–7
exercises, 100–101, 105
fair, 100, 103
"gunny-sacking" in, 100
productive, 101
repetitive, 102
rules for, 103
Fihran, Harlman F., *Treatment of Sexual Dysfunction*, 79
friends and friendship, 219–34
  boundaries in, 230
  case histories, 226–27
  contracts about, 243, 246–47
  as couple, 230–34
  differing needs in, 219, 222–24
  exercises, 223, 224–25, 228–29, 230–33
  meaning of, 219–21
  outside marriage, 226–30
  partners as, 221–22
  role differences in, 219
  transitory nature of, 223–24
  "true," 224–26
frigidity, 133–34

grandchildren, 218

husband. *See* Marriage; Roles and role concepts

impotence, 122–23
in-laws. *See* Relatives

journal keeping, as self-awareness tool, 85

Koestenbaum, Peter, *Existential Sexuality: Choosing to Love*, 142

Lakein, Alan, *How to Get Control of Your Time and Your Life*, 163

Index

love:
  commitment in, 129–30
  as conquering all, 5–6
  daily decision in, 7
  deprivation as cause of insecurity in, 13
  impulsive buying as substitute for, 189–90
  intimacy and empathy in, 129–32
  money as substitute for, 175, 180–81
  myths about, 5, 6
  nourishment necessary for, 6–7.
  See also Children; Marriage; Sex

marital check-up, 54–81, 259–60
  communication exercise, 76–77
  conflict summary, 80–81
  dyadic adjustment scale, 65–66
  interpersonal comparison tests, 69–73
  listening and role reversal, 73–74
  marital appraisal, 67–69
  reasons for, 55–56
  relaxation exercises for, 57
  self-disclosure exercise, 58–61
  self-liking exercise, 61–65
  sexual relations inventory, 78–80
  taking direction, 73–74
  time priorities and management exercise, 77–78
  yes–no inventory, 75–76
marriage:
  acceptance of partner in, 25, 29
  accommodation in, 106–7
  assertion in, 88, 106
  body language in, 83, 87, 90, 92–93, 138
  boredom in, 138–39
  commitment in, 19, 20, 22
  communication in, 61–62, 65, 83–94
  companionship in, 15
  compromise in, 23–25, 32, 94–109
  conflicts and conflict resolution in, 11–12, 27–28, 30, 32, 94–109, 186
  connectedness in, 19
  creative, 19
  crisis management in, 253–55
  disagreement negotiation in, 24, 94–109
  distance necessary in, 102–3, 160–61
  emotional insecurity in, 17–18
  equality in, 19, 20
  as escape, 13–14
  exclusivity in, 19
  expectations in, 15, 31
  experience as teacher in, 3–4
  expression of feelings in, 22, 90–91
  fighting in, 11–12, 100–109
  healthy, 12, 15
  honesty in, 27, 30, 88–90
  ignorance about, 3–4
  intellectual insecurity in, 18–19, 88–90
  interaction in, 64–66
  intimacy in, 15, 19, 105, 129–32, 135–36, 163–64, 203–4, 215
  irrationality in, 11–12
  listening in, 73–74, 90
  love fluctuations in, 19–20
  low self-esteem in, 13–14, 16
  material dependence and insecurity in, 16–17, 49
  mating gradient in, 17–18
  mini-contracts in, 29–31, 35

INDEX

marriage (*Continued*)
  mood swings in, 19–20
  need fulfillment in, 21–22
  negative feelings in, 27–28
  negotiating in, 94–109
  obligations in, 15–16
  as obsolete, 3
  permanence in, 19
  professional help for, 250–52
  realities of, 15–37
  relatives, problems with, 167
  resentments in, 107, 109
  romance vs. reality in, 15
  scripts in, 28, 31
  second, 179
  security in, 15, 16, 42
  self-awareness and self-knowledge in, 83–84, 85–87
  sexual exclusivity in, 22
  silent treatment in, 108–9
  skills necessary in, 26, 28, 29, 30, 39
  stability in, 19
  time conflicts and resolution in, 165–70
  time use in, 155–73
  trivial complaints in, 23–25, 35
  unrealistic expectations in, 4–5, 31, 32
  vacation from, 103
  vulnerability in, 19, 103, 251
  work necessary in, 26, 29–30
  See also Children; Exercises; Friends and Friendship; Love; Marital check-up; Marriage myths; Marriage styles; Money; Roles and role concepts; Values
marriage myths, 3–14, 31
  case histories, 32–34
  constant excitement, 8–9
  constant happiness, 4
  exercise, 34–37
  fighting as irrational, 11–12
  love conquers all, 5–7
  "normal" as goal, 12
  and role concepts, 5
  sexual perfection, 7–8
  total fulfillment, 40–43
  total harmony, 9–10
  worthlessness feelings removed, 13–14
marriage styles, 38–53
  as composite, 38
  "dead," 49–50, 52, 105–7
  evaluation exercise, 50–53
  freedom to examine, 38–39
  fulfilled marriage, 40–43, 52
  gradual change in, 53–53
  limited partnership, 43–49, 52
Miller, Sherod, Nunnally, Ilam W., and Wackman, Daniel B., *Alive and Aware: How to Improve Your Relationship Through Better Communication*, 85–86
mini-contracts, 29–31, 35, 188, 243–47
  with children, 207, 212.
  See also Contracts and contract negotiating
money and money management, 174–90
  agreement about, 181–82, 183–84
  budgeting, 186–88
  case histories, 174–75, 182–83, 184–85, 186–88
  for charity, 175, 182–83
  contracts in, 243–44
  credit buying, 189
  exercise, 185–86
  for the good life, 175, 181–82
  as love substitute, 175, 180–81, 189–90
  as nest egg, 175, 183–85
  as possession and control, 175, 177–79

Index

money and money management (*Continued*)
  as power, 175, 176–77
  as security, 175, 179–80
  separate accounts, 179
Myers, Karen and Porat, Frieda, *Changing Your Lifestyle*, 20, 39

natural childbirth, 197

O'Neill, George and O'Neill, Nena, *Open Marriage*, 44

parenthood. *See* Children
Phillips, Alice and Smith, Gerald, *Me, You and Us*, 102–3, 137–38
Porat, Frieda and Myers, Karen, *Changing Your Lifestyle*, 20, 39
premature ejaculation, 123–24
professional help, 250–52, 258, 259

quizzes. *See* Exercises

Raths, Louis, 148
relatives, problems with, 166–70
role playing, 139
roles and role concepts, 5, 45
  changes in, 110–11
  in child care, 200–1, 243, 245–46
  in "dead" marriage, 49–50
  in friendships, 219
  "good husband," 28, 32, 42
  "good wife," 7, 28, 32, 42
  in household management, 243, 244–45
  husband's contribution necessary, 7
  in limited marriage, 47–48
  "nice guy," 107–8
  in professional life, 243, 247
  in sex, 116–17
  "strong man," 18–19
  traditional, 16–17, 18, 111, 177–78

self-awareness and self-knowledge, 58–61, 83–84, 85–87
sex, 110–39
  anxiety in, 8
  attitude changes about, 111
  boredom in, 138–39
  conditions on, 120–21
  in "dead" marriage, 49
  exclusivity in marriage, 22
  exercises, 78–80, 117, 126–27, 129, 134–35
  extramarital, 44–46, 115, 124–26, 254–55
  female orgasm in, 114–15, 121, 133–34
  frequency of, 118–19
  frigidity, 133
  impotence, 122–23
  orgasm in, 114–15, 121
  premature ejaculation, 123–24
  quality vs. frequency of, 8, 118–19
  reciprocation in, 137–38
  roles, 116–17, 119
  touching and, 137
  variety in, 120
  as weapon, 120
  See also Sexual myths
sexual myths, 112–15
  anxiety caused by, 8
  constant perfection, 32
  erection necessary, 113
  man as initiator, 112
  as man's need, 112
  man's responsibility for woman's pleasure, 113, 114
  monogamy, 115
  one way to reach orgasm, 114

sexual myths (*Continued*)
  "producing on demand," 8, 113
  simultaneous orgasm, 114–15
  woman as judge of lovemaking, 114, 115
  woman's coyness, 112–13
  woman's duty, 112
silent treatment, 108–9
Simon, Sidney H., Howe, Leland W. and Kirschenbaum, Howard, *Values Clarification*, 148
Smith, Gerald and Phillips, Alice, *Me, You and Us*, 102–3, 137–38

values, 140–54
  case histories, 140–41, 146–47, 148–49
  children, 144–45
  conflict and conflict resolution, 11–42, 143, 150–54
  entertainment, 145–46
  exercises, 143–46, 154
  friends, 145
  home, 145
  identification of, 142–43
  and meaning, 141–42
  money, 144
  priorities in, 152–53
  time, 144
  valuing process, 148–50
  work, 144

wife. *See* Marriage; Roles and role concepts; Women's liberation movement
women's liberation movement, 17, 18, 110
worthlessness and low self-esteem, feelings of, 13, 16
Wyden, Peter and Bach, George, *Intimate Enemy: Creative Aggression, The*, 55